The Cheeky Wee Monkey Joke Book

The Cheeky Wee Monkey Joke Book

THE BEST SCOTTISH CHILDREN'S JOKE BOOK EVER

ALLAN MORRISON

BLACK & WHITE PUBLISHING

First published 2008
by Black & White Publishing Ltd
29 Ocean Drive, Edinburgh EH6 6JL

1 3 5 7 9 10 8 6 4 2 08 09 10 11 12

ISBN: 978 1 84502 226 6

A CIP catalogue record for this book is available from the British Library.

Typeset by RefineCatch Limited, Bungay, Suffolk
Printed and bound by Norhaven A/S, Denmark

THE CHEEKY WEE MONKEY JOKE BOOK!

If you're a cheeky wee monkey, a clever wee monkey, a crafty wee monkey, a tricky wee monkey, or even a . . . cheeky, clever, crafty and tricky wee monkey, then THIS IS THE JOKE BOOK FOR YOU. Try them out on your pals, your brothers and sisters, your parents, but watch which ones you tell grandma!

You don't monkey around with Cheeky Wee Monkey. He's the smartest primate around. Always likes the last word, mischievous and is forever up to monkey business.

And jings, unlike other monkeys . . . he's Scottish!

Dedicated to my own cheeky wee monkeys:
Charlie, Finlay, Isabella and Rory

CONTENTS

S . . . KOOL JOKES

Teacher: What do you call someone who keeps on talking when people are no longer interested?
Cheeky Wee Monkey: A teacher, miss!

Teacher: Poet Robert Burns had to walk five miles to school every day.
Cheeky Wee Monkey: Well, he should have waited and got the school bus, miss!

Teacher: Poet Robert Burns wrote 'To a Mouse'.
Cheeky Wee Monkey: Ah bet he didnae get a reply, miss!

Teacher: Where did the Vikings land when they came to Scotland?
Cheeky Wee Monkey: On their feet, miss!

Teacher: Did you know that it takes three Scottish sheep to make a sweater?
Cheeky Wee Monkey: Ah didnae even know Scottish sheep could knit, miss!

Teacher: Why did the Romans build so many straight roads in Scotland?
Cheeky Wee Monkey: So that their soldiers wouldn't go roon the bend, miss!

Teacher: Who succeeded the first Scottish king?
Cheeky Wee Monkey: The second wan, miss!

Teacher: In the olden days did the Scots hunt bear?
Cheeky Wee Monkey: Probably no' in the winter, miss!

Teacher: Name an animal found in Scotland.
Cheeky Wee Monkey: A deer, miss!

Teacher: Good, now name one more.
Cheeky Wee Monkey: Another deer, miss!

Teacher: What is the difference between unlawful and illegal?
Cheeky Wee Monkey: Unlawful is doing something wrong. Illegal is a sick bird found in the north o' Scotland, miss!

Teacher: If a man dies in England who was born in Scotland, brought up in America, worked in Spain and married in Australia, what is he?
Cheeky Wee Monkey: Dead, miss!

Teacher: What came after the stone age and the iron age?
Cheeky Wee Monkey: The saus-age, miss!

Teacher: Name five animals that live in Edinburgh Zoo.
Cheeky Wee Monkey: A lion an' four elephants, miss!

Teacher: Name three famous Poles.
Cheeky Wee Monkey: North, South and tad, miss!

Teacher: Where was the Declaration of Arbroath signed?
Cheeky Wee Monkey: At the bottom, miss!

Teacher: Name the four seasons.
Cheeky Wee Monkey: Salt, pepper, fitba' and cricket, miss!

Teacher: Do Eskimos eat whale meat and blubber?
Cheeky Wee Monkey: Well miss, if ah had to eat whale meat ah'd blubber, tae!

Teacher: Where is the English Channel?
Cheeky Wee Monkey: Probably jist after Channel 4 and Channel 5, miss?

Teacher: What is your favourite Scottish food?
Cheeky Wee Monkey: Seconds, miss!

Teacher: Please give me a long sentence.
Cheeky Wee Monkey: 'Life imprisonment', miss!

Teacher: I just wish you'd pay a little attention!
Cheeky Wee Monkey: Miss, ah'm paying as little as ah can!

Teacher: What happened after the wheel was invented?
Cheeky Wee Monkey: It probably caused a revolution, miss!

Teacher: I see that one of your socks is white and the other is red.
Cheeky Wee Monkey: Aye, and I've got a pair just like it at home, miss!

Teacher: Did your parents help you with your homework?
Cheeky Wee Monkey: No, ah got it wrong masel', miss!

Teacher: If there are six flies on a window and I swat one, how many will be left?
Cheeky Wee Monkey: Jist the dead wan, miss!

Teacher: How does a blacksmith shoe a horse?
Cheeky Wee Monkey: He jist looks him in the eye miss, an' says, 'Shoo, shoo!'

Teacher: Who can tell me the purpose of a school?
Cheeky Wee Monkey: Without school there would be no school holidays, miss!

Teacher: What is the plural of child?
Cheeky Wee Monkey: Twins, miss!

Teacher: What is a volcano?
Cheeky Wee Monkey: A mountain with hiccups, miss!

Teacher: If you were to add 89 and 94 what would you get?
Cheeky Wee Monkey: The wrang answer, miss!

Teacher: How do you stop milk turning sour?
Cheeky Wee Monkey: Keep it in the coo, miss!

Teacher: Name one fantastic thing we have today that we didn't have ten years ago?
Cheeky Wee Monkey: Me, miss!

Teacher: Which city cheats during exams?
Cheeky Wee Monkey: Peking, miss!

Teacher: Why are you doing your sums on the floor?
Cheeky Wee Monkey: Please miss, you told me to dae them without using tables!

Teacher: You missed school yesterday, didn't you?
Cheeky Wee Monkey: Not a bit, miss!

Teacher: I'm worried that you're always bottom of the class.
Cheeky Wee Monkey: Don't worry, miss. You teach the same stuff at both ends!

Teacher: Why did early man draw pictures of hippopotamuses and rhinoceroses on the walls of their caves?
Cheeky Wee Monkey: Because they couldnae spell their names!

Teacher: How many bridges does Edinburgh have?
Cheeky Wee Monkey: Four, miss.

Teacher: How can there possibly be four?
Cheeky Wee Monkey: Well, last week ma daddy drove over the Forth Bridge, miss!

Teacher: What is the capital of Scotland?
Cheeky Wee Monkey: 'S', miss!

Teacher: What does www stand for on the internet?
Cheeky Wee Monkey: Wee Willie Winkie, miss!

Teacher: Give me three collective nouns.
Cheeky Wee Monkey: Flypaper, a wheely-bin an' a vacuum cleaner, miss!

Teacher: Who sometimes lives in a monastery?
Cheeky Wee Monkey: The Loch Ness Monster, miss!

Teacher: What are the small rivers called that run into the Nile?
Cheeky Wee Monkey: The juveniles, miss!

Teacher: What is an operetta?
Cheeky Wee Monkey: A person who works for a phone company, miss!

Teacher: What does minimum mean?
Cheeky Wee Monkey: A wee mummy, miss!

Teacher: What was the name of the Greek mythological creature that was half man and half animal?
Cheeky Wee Monkey: Buffalo Bill, miss!

Teacher: You've got your shoes on the wrong feet.
Cheeky Wee Monkey: Please miss, they're the only feet ah have!

Teacher: Use the word 'diploma' in a sentence.
Cheeky Wee Monkey: If there is a water leak you phone diploma, miss!

Teacher: Why are you always late?
Cheeky Wee Monkey: Well miss, when I get near tae the school there's a big notice that says, 'go slow'!

Teacher: You must write legibly.
Cheeky Wee Monkey: But miss, then you'll know ah cannae spell!

Teacher: What is the purpose of an alarm clock?
Cheeky Wee Monkey: To wake people who have nae children, miss!

Teacher: What is a traffic jam?
Cheeky Wee Monkey: Something that's spread over Scottish streets every night, miss!

Teacher: Didn't you know the school bell has gone?
Cheeky Wee Monkey: Well, ah didnae take it, miss!

Teacher: What do they do in Aberdeen with crude oil?
Cheeky Wee Monkey: Teach it manners, miss!

Teacher: What is cowhide used for?
Cheeky Wee Monkey: To keep the coo in, miss!

Teacher: If I cut two apples into ten pieces and two pears into ten pieces, what will I get?
Cheeky Wee Monkey: A fruit salad, miss!

Teacher: What is a Fjord?
Cheeky Wee Monkey: A car made in Norway, miss!

Teacher: What do I mean when I say the 'plural' of something?
Cheeky Wee Monkey: The same thing, but only more of it, miss!

Teacher: I like to be very fair to everyone. I would never tell anyone off for something they did not do.
Cheeky Wee Monkey: Thank goodness, miss. I didnae do my homework!

Teacher: Today we will talk about planets and meteorites. Name a star with a tail?
Cheeky Wee Monkey: Mickey Mouse, miss!

Teacher: Who invented fire?
Cheeky Wee Monkey: Some bright spark, miss!

Teacher: How can you prevent diseases caused by biting snakes?
Cheeky Wee Monkey: Don't bite any, miss!

Teacher: Name two birds which cannot fly.
Cheeky Wee Monkey: An ostrich an' a dead seagull, miss!

Teacher: If I had six apples in one hand and seven apples in the other what would I have?
Cheeky Wee Monkey: Big hands, miss!

Teacher: What are tulips?
Cheeky Wee Monkey: What everybody has roon their mouth, miss!

Teacher: When you yawn you should put your hand in front of your mouth.
Cheeky Wee Monkey: But ah might get bitten, miss!

Teacher: Do you think there is one word in our language that contains all the vowels?
Cheeky Wee Monkey: Unquestionably, miss!

Teacher: What's the difference between a Scottish school pupil and an Australian school pupil?
Cheeky Wee Monkey: About twelve thousand miles, miss!

Teacher: Please spell 'weather'.
Cheeky Wee Monkey: 'W-e-v-v-u-r'.
Teacher: That's probably the worst spell of weather we've ever had in Scotland!

Teacher: Today I want you to write something on Hadrian's Wall.
Cheeky Wee Monkey: Please miss, can ah just use a bit of paper?

Teacher: You aren't paying attention to me. Are you having trouble hearing?
Cheeky Wee Monkey: No, listening, miss!

Teacher: What do you mean you ate your homework?
Cheeky Wee Monkey: Well miss, you said it wis a piece of cake!

Teacher: Your homework seems to be in your father's handwriting.
Cheeky Wee Monkey: Aye miss, ah used his pen!

Teacher: Why do polar bears have fur coats?
Cheeky Wee Monkey: Because they'd look silly in anoraks, miss!

Teacher: Remember, school blazers are required to eat in the school dining hall.
Cheeky Wee Monkey: Where dae the pupils eat, miss?

Teacher: What is a myth?
Cheeky Wee Monkey: An unmarried lady, miss!

Teacher: Have you ever seen a six foot snake?
Cheeky Wee Monkey: Miss, a snake doesnae have any feet!

Teacher: What do the French eat in Paris for puddings?
Cheeky Wee Monkey: The Trifle Tower, miss!

Teacher: I hope I didn't see you looking at Isabella's exam paper.
Cheeky Wee Monkey: Ah hope you didn't see me either, miss!

Teacher: Today we will do history. Who can tell me who followed Mary the First?
Cheeky Wee Monkey: Her little lamb, miss!

Teacher: Didn't you hear me call you?
Cheeky Wee Monkey: But you said not to answer you back, miss!

Teacher: Have you ever seen a duchess?
Cheeky Wee Monkey: Aye, it's the same as an English 'S', miss!

Teacher: Why are you always a bit dirty?
Cheeky Wee Monkey: Well I'm a bit closer tae the ground than you are, miss!

Teacher: Were the pyramids built by the Egyptians?
Cheeky Wee Monkey: I sphinx so, miss!

Teacher: Where is Hadrian's Wall?
Cheeky Wee Monkey: Roon wee Hadrian's garden, miss!

Teacher: Use the word 'fascinate' in a sentence.
Cheeky Wee Monkey: I have a coat with nine buttons, but I can only fascinate, miss!

Daddy: What did you learn in school today?
Cheeky Wee Monkey: Ah learned that the homework you helped me with was wrong!

Teacher: Why is Russia now a fast moving country?
Cheeky Wee Monkey: Because the people are always Russian, miss!

Teacher: How many seconds are there in a year?
Cheeky Wee Monkey: Twelve, miss. The second of January, the second of February, the second . . . !

Teacher: Why did Robin Hood steal from the rich?
Cheeky Wee Monkey: Because the poor didn't have anything he could steal, miss!

Teacher: What colour would you paint the sun and the wind?
Cheeky Wee Monkey: The sun rose and the wind blue, miss!

Why did the maths teacher take a ruler to bed with her?
Cheeky Wee Monkey: She wanted tae see how long she would sleep, miss!

Why did the nose not want to go to school?
Cheeky Wee Monkey: He wis tired of being picked on!

How do you like going to school?
Cheeky Wee Monkey: The going bit and the coming home bit are fine. Ah'm no' too keen on the bit in between!

Teacher: How do you manage to get so many things wrong?
Cheeky Wee Monkey: Ah start early, miss!

Daddy: What did you learn in school today?
Cheeky Wee Monkey: Not enough. I've got tae go back tomorrow!

Why are schools never beside chicken farms?
Cheeky Wee Monkey: So that pupils don't hear fowl language!

Cheeky Wee Monkey: You must love me, miss.
Teacher: And why do you think that?
Cheeky Wee Monkey: You keep putting kisses beside my sums!

Do you know what happened when Cheeky Wee Monkey tied all the pupils' shoelaces in his class together?
They all went on a school trip!

JOKES TO SCARE YOU! (OH, MUMMY, DADDY!)

What do you call a fierce monster with no neck?
Cheeky Wee Monkey: The Lost Neck Monster.

What's it like to be kissed by a vampire?
Cheeky Wee Monkey: It's a pain in the neck!

What did the nurse say to the witch?
Cheeky Wee Monkey: You can get up this efternoon for a spell!

Where do ghosts mail their letters?
Cheeky Wee Monkey: At the Ghost Office!

What happens to angry witches when they ride their broomsticks?
Cheeky Wee Monkey: They fly aff the handle!

What did the daddy ghost say to the baby ghost?
Cheeky Wee Monkey: Only spook when yer spooken to!

Why can't skeletons lie?
Cheeky Wee Monkey: Because people can see right through them!

What exam do witches have to pass?
Cheeky Wee Monkey: Spell-ing tests!

What does a ghost use to go haunting?
Cheeky Wee Monkey: Boos and arrows!

What kind of a dog has Dracula?
Cheeky Wee Monkey: A blood hound!

Why are vampires thin?
Cheeky Wee Monkey: They eat necks to nothing!

What do skeletons say when they start eating?
Cheeky Wee Monkey: Bone-appetit!

How do witches lose weight?
Cheeky Wee Monkey: They join Weight Witches!

Why did the skeleton laugh?
Cheeky Wee Monkey: Because he had a funny bone!

Where do baby ghosts go during the day?
Cheeky Wee Monkey: Dayscare centres!

What do you get if you cross a ghost with the Loch Ness Monster?
Cheeky Wee Monkey: Something that is very seldom seen!

What do baby ghosts wear on their feet?
Cheeky Wee Monkey: Boo-ties!

What do you call a baby ghost's mummy and daddy?
Cheeky Wee Monkey: Transparents!

What game do ghosts like best?
Cheeky Wee Monkey: Hide and Shriek!

What do you call a skeleton who won't get out of bed in the morning?
Cheeky Wee Monkey: A lazy bones!

What is a ghost's favourite type of tie?
Cheeky Wee Monkey: A boo-tie!

What do you call a ghost with a sore leg?
Cheeky Wee Monkey: A hoblin goblin!

Why do you find so many Scottish ghosts in pubs?
Cheeky Wee Monkey: They like their boos!

What streets do ghosts haunt?
Cheeky Wee Monkey: Dead ends!

Why couldn't the witch sing?
Cheeky Wee Monkey: Because she had a frog in her throat!

What is evil and horrible inside and green outside?
Cheeky Wee Monkey: A witch dressed as a cucumber!

What do you get when you cross a ghost with a boy scout?
Cheeky Wee Monkey: Someone who frightens old ladies across the road!

What do you get if you cross a ghost with a packet of crisps?
Cheeky Wee Monkey: Snacks that go crunch in the night!

How did the witch know she was ill?
Cheeky Wee Monkey: She had a dizzy spell!

Why was the skeleton frightened?
Cheeky Wee Monkey: He had nae guts!

What is Dracula's favourite soup?
Cheeky Wee Monkey: Scream o' tomato!

Who does Dracula get letters from?
Cheeky Wee Monkey: His fang club!

Who did Dracula invite to his party?
Cheeky Wee Monkey: Anyone he could dig up!

Why is Dracula an artist?
Cheeky Wee Monkey: Because he likes to draw blood.

Why does Dracula have no friends?
Cheeky Wee Monkey: Because he's a pain in the neck!

Why does Dracula take cough mixture?
Cheeky Wee Monkey: To stop his coffin!

Why do demons and ghouls go out together?
Cheeky Wee Monkey: Cause demons are a ghoul's best friend!

What do you call a ghost who gets too close to a fire?
Cheeky Wee Monkey: A toasty ghosty!

What do ghosts eat at lunch?
Cheeky Wee Monkey: Spookgetti!

What goes cackle cackle splat?
Cheeky Wee Monkey: A witch flying her broomstick into Ben Nevis!

What do you call a witch who lives on a beach?
Cheeky Wee Monkey: A sand-witch!

How do witches tell the time?
Cheeky Wee Monkey: They look at their witch watch.

What did the witch ask for when she went into her holiday hotel?
Cheeky Wee Monkey: A broom with a view!

What do you call a witch's garage?
Cheeky Wee Monkey: A broom cupboard!

What's a witch's favourite ride at the fair?
Cheeky Wee Monkey: The ghost train!

Where does Dracula swim?
Cheeky Wee Monkey: In the Dead Sea!

How do you know a vampire likes table tennis?
Cheeky Wee Monkey: Every night he turns into a bat!

What happened when the ghost asked in a pub for a whisky?
Cheeky Wee Monkey: The barman said he didn't serve spirits!

Why didn't the skeleton go to the dance?
Cheeky Wee Monkey: He had nae-body to go with!

Why did the skeleton go into the restaurant?
Cheeky Wee Monkey: He was looking fur spare ribs!

Why do witches wear pointy hats?
Cheeky Wee Monkey: To keep their pointy heads warm!

Have you heard of a good weather witch?
Cheeky Wee Monkey: Aye. We should have wan in Scotland because they forecast sunny spells!

What musical instrument do skeletons play?
Cheeky Wee Monkey: The trombone!

Why didn't the boy spirit ask the girl spirit out?
Cheeky Wee Monkey: He thought he didn't stand a ghost of a chance!

What can't you give a headless ghost?
Cheeky Wee Monkey: A headache!

How can you tell when a witch is really ugly?
Cheeky Wee Monkey: When a bee stings her it closes its eyes!

What do you get if you cross Bambi with a ghost?
Cheeky Wee Monkey: Bamboo!

What do schools do to naughty witches?
Cheeky Wee Monkey: They ex-pell them!

Why wasn't there much food left after the monster party?
Cheeky Wee Monkey: Because everyone was a goblin!

Why are witches like candles?
Cheeky Wee Monkey: They are wick-ed!

What's a ghost's favourite pudding?
Cheeky Wee Monkey: Boo-berry pie!

What do ghosts serve for pudding?
Cheeky Wee Monkey: I scream!

If Dracula knocks you out in a boxing match, what are you?
Cheeky Wee Monkey: Out for the Count!

Why are ghosts messy eaters?
Cheeky Wee Monkey: Because they're always goblin!

What noise does a witch's car make?
Cheeky Wee Monkey: Broom, broom, broom!

Why do witches wear badges with their names printed on them?
Cheeky Wee Monkey: So people will know which witch is which!

What do witches put on their hair?
Cheeky Wee Monkey: Scare spray!

What do you call two witches living together?
Cheeky Wee Monkey: Broom-mates!

MONKEY JOKES!

What's a monkey's favourite girl pop group?
Cheeky Wee Monkey: Bananarama!

What is a monkey's favourite gymnastic trick?
Cheeky Wee Monkey: Doin' a banana split!

What do you get if you cross an ape with a seafood shop?
Cheeky Wee Monkey: Fish and chimps!

Does a monkey like to fly?
Cheeky Wee Monkey: Aye, in hot air baboons!

What is yellow and brown, yellow and brown, yellow and brown?
Cheeky Wee Monkey: A monkey rolling doon a hill holding a banana!

Who's the smelliest ape in the world?
Cheeky Wee Monkey: King Pong!

Why did the monkey cross the road?
Cheeky Wee Monkey: The chicken wis away on holiday!

What is a monkey's favourite flower?
Cheeky Wee Monkey: A chimp-ansy!

Can a monkey jump higher than Edinburgh Castle?
Cheeky Wee Monkey: Aye, Edinburgh Castle can't jump!

Why do monkeys scratch themselves?
Cheeky Wee Monkey: Because we're the only wans who know where the itch is!

What kind of key does a monkey use to open a banana?
Cheeky Wee Monkey: A monk-key!

What do you call a monkey who is a wizard at snooker?
Cheeky Wee Monkey: Hairy Potter!

Why did the monkey's banana go to the doctor?
Cheeky Wee Monkey: Because he wisnae peeling well!

What carol does a monkey sing?
Cheeky Wee Monkey: Jungle bells!

How does a monkey get downstairs?
Cheeky Wee Monkey: He slides doon the banana-ster!

What day does a monkey like best?
Cheeky Wee Monkey: Ape-ril Fools Day!

What do you call a bad tempered gorilla?
Cheeky Wee Monkey: Sir!

Why do gorillas have large nostrils?
Cheeky Wee Monkey: Because they have large fingers!

Where does a twenty stones gorilla sleep?
Cheeky Wee Monkey: Anywhere he likes!

Where do baby monkeys sleep?
Cheeky Wee Monkey: In Ape-ri-cots!

Why don't monkeys in the jungle play at cards?
Cheeky Wee Monkey: There are too many cheetahs!

What do you call a monkey who works in a call centre?
Cheeky Wee Monkey: A who-rang-utang!

What did the banana say to the cheeky wee monkey?
Cheeky Wee Monkey: Nothing, bananas cannae talk!

Why don't apes tell stories?
Cheeky Wee Monkey: Because they have no tales!

Where do monkeys buy their clothes?
Cheeky Wee Monkey: At jungle sales!

KNOCK, KNOCK JOKES

Knock, knock.
Who's there?
Big Ish.
Big Ish who?
Not today, thanks!

Knock, knock.
Who's there?
Al.
Al who?
Al give you a wee kiss if you open the door!

Knock, knock.
Who's there?
Leaf.
Leaf who?
Leaf me alone!

Knock, knock.
Who's there?
Doughnut
Doughnut who?
Doughnut answer the door to strangers!

Knock, knock.
Who's there?
Turnip.
Turnip who?
Turnip the heating, it's freezing!

Knock, knock.
Who's there?
Diploma.
Diploma who?
Diploma is here to fix your leak!

Knock, knock.
Who's there?
Tank.
Tank who?
You're welcome!

Knock, knock.
Who's there?
Romeo.
Romeo who?
Romeo over the river, would you?

Knock, knock.
Who's there?
Juliette.
Juliette who?
Juliette all my chips!

Knock, knock.
Who's there?
Repeat.
Repeat who?
Okay. Who, who, who, who, who!

Knock, knock.
Who's there?
Freeze.
Freeze who?
Freeze a jolly good fellow!

Knock, knock.
Who's there?
Noah.
Noah who?
Noah accounting for taste!

Knock, knock.
Who's there?
Lucy.
Lucy who?
There's Lucy lastic in my panties!

Knock, knock.
Who's there?
Scott.
Scott who?
Scott nothing to do with you!

Knock, knock.
Who's there?
Omelette.
Omelette who?
Omelette smarter than I look!

Knock, knock.
Who's there?
A wee boy who can't reach the doorbell!

Knock, knock.
Who's there?
Lettuce.
Lettuce who?
Lettuce play on your piano!

Knock, knock.
Who's there?
Dinny.
Dinny who?
Dinny talk with your mouth full!

Knock, knock.
Who's there?
Too whit.
Too whit who?
Is there an owl in this house?

Knock, knock.
Who's there?
Gestapo.
Gestapo who?
Ve ask the questions!

Knock, knock.
Who's there?
Hawaii.
Hawaii who?
I'm fine. Hawaii you?

Knock, knock.
Who's there?
Wanty.
Wanty who?
Wanty have another guess?

Knock, knock.
Who's there?
Figs.
Figs who?
Figs your doorbell, it's broken!

Knock, knock.
Who's there?
Cows.
Cows who?
No they don't, they moo!

Knock, knock.
Who's there?
Rosa.
Rosa who?
Rosa wee houses!

Knock, knock.
Who's there?
Annie.
Annie who?
Annie thing you can do, I can do better!

Knock, knock.
Who's there?
Tom.
Tom who?
Tom on, you know who I am!

Knock, knock.
Who's there?
Justin.
Justin who?
Just in time for tea!

Knock, knock.
Who's there?
Boo.
Boo who?
Well, you don't have to cry about it!

Knock, knock.
Who's there?
Tank.
Tank who?
Tank me for what?

Knock, knock.
Who's there?
Bin.
Bin who?
Bin anywhere nice lately?

Knock, knock.
Who's there?
July.
July who?
July or do you tell the truth?

Knock, knock.
Who's there?
Butter.
Butter who?
Butter hurry up . . . I need the loo!

Knock, knock.
Who's there?
Neil.
Neil who?
Neil down, it's the Queen!

Knock, knock.
Who's there?
Moo.
Moo who?
Well make up your mind. Are you a cow or an owl?

Knock, knock.
Who's there?
Anita.
Anita who?
Anita use your loo!

Knock, knock.
Who's there?
Doctor.
Doctor Who?
Oh, I just love your programme, doctor!

Knock, knock.
Who's there?
Shelby.
Shelby who?
Shelby coming round the mountain when she comes!

Knock, knock.
Who's there?
Art.
Art who?
R2, D2!

Knock, knock.
Who's there?
Freddie.
Freddie who?
Freddie or not, here I come!

Knock, knock.
Who's there?
Wendy.
Wendy who?
Wendy red red robin comes bob bob bobbin' along!

Knock, knock.
Who's there?
Police.
Police who?
Police let us in, it's cold out here!

Knock, knock.
Who's there?
Olive.
Olive who?
Olive you!

Knock, knock.
Who's there?
You who.
You who who.
You're a good yodeller!

Knock, knock.
Who's there?
Amos.
Amos who?
A mosquito!

Knock, knock.
Who's there?
Consumption.
Consumption who?
Consumption not be done about that mosquito?

Knock, knock.
Who's there?
Frank.
Frank who?
Frank you for being my friend!

Knock, knock.
Who's there?
Athena.
Athena who?
Athena a great film yesterday!

Knock, knock.
Who's there?
Alec.
Alec who?
Alec-tricity – isn't it shocking!

Knock, knock.
Who's there?
Canoe.
Canoe who?
Canoe come out to play?

Knock, knock.
Who's there?
Anida.
Anida who?
Anida wee . . . where's your loo?

Knock, knock.
Who's there?
Pooch.
Pooch who?
Pooch your arms around me and give me a kiss.

Knock, knock.
Who's there?
Tinker Bell.
Tinker Bell who?
Tinker Bell isn't working!

Knock, knock.
Who's there?
Atish.
Atish who?
Bless you!

Knock, knock.
Who's there?
Thistle.
Thistle who?
Thistle have to do you until tea is ready!

Knock, knock.
Who's there?
Arthur.
Arthur who?
Arthur any sweeties left?

Knock, Knock.
Who's there?
Ice cream soda.
Ice cream soda who?
Ice cream soda people can hear me!

Knock, knock.
Who's there?
Norma Lee.
Norma Lee who?
Norma Lee I let myself in but I've forgotten my keys.

Knock, knock.
Who's there?
Dishes.
Dishes who?
Dishes the police. Come out with your hands up!

Knock, knock.
Who's there?
Howard.
Howard who?
I'm fine, Howard you?

Knock, knock.
Who's there?
Abee.
Abee who?
ABCDEFGHIJ . . . . !

Knock, knock.
Who's there?
Luke.
Luke who?
Luke through the keyhole and you'll find out!

Knock, knock.
Who's there?
Gizza.
Gizza who?
Gizza wee kiss!

Knock, knock.
Who's there?
Nobel.
Nobel who?
No bell, that's why I knocked!

Would you remember me in a week?
Yes.
Would you remember me in a month?
Yes.
Would you remember me in a year?
Yes.
Knock, knock.
Who's there?
I thought you said you would remember me!

Knock, knock.
Who's there?
Heaven.
Heaven who?
Heaven you heard enough knock-knock jokes?

'AWAY WITH THE BIRDS' JOKES!

Why do birds in Scotland fly south for the winter?
Cheeky Wee Monkey: Because it's too far to walk!

Where do one-eyed birds shop?
Cheeky Wee Monkey: The Birds Eye shop!

Can woodpeckers speak?
Cheeky Wee Monkey: No, but most know Morse code!

What is bright red and sounds like a parrot?
Cheeky Wee Monkey: A carrot!

What do you get if you cross a hen with a guitar?
Cheeky Wee Monkey: A hen that plays when you pluck it!

What do you get if you cross a cockerel and a duck?
Cheeky Wee Monkey: A bird that gets up at the quack of dawn!

What do you get if you cross a carrier pigeon with a woodpecker?
Cheeky Wee Monkey: A bird that can carry a message and is able to knock on the door when it arrives!

Where do tough chickens come from?
Cheeky Wee Monkey: Hard boiled eggs!

What do you call a woodpecker with no beak?
Cheeky Wee Monkey: A headbanger!

What do you sing to your budgie on its birthday?
Cheeky Wee Monkey: Happy birdy to you!

What do you get if you cross a hyena and a parrot?
Cheeky Wee Monkey: An animal that can tell you whit it's laughing at!

What do you get if you cross a pig with a parrot?
Cheeky Wee Monkey: A bird who hogs the conversation!

Why do hummingbirds hum?
Cheeky Wee Monkey: Because they cannae remember the words!

What do you call a Scotsman who marries a chicken?
Cheeky Wee Monkey: Henpecked!

Why does a flamingo stand on one leg?
Cheeky Wee Monkey: Because if it lifted up both legs it would fall doon!

What do you get if you put a budgie in a blender?
Cheeky Wee Monkey: Shredded tweet!

What do you get if you cross a homing pigeon with a parrot?
Cheeky Wee Monkey: A bird that can ask the way if it gets lost!

What's yellow and hops up and down?
Cheeky Wee Monkey: A canary wi' hiccups!

What birds are always out of breath?
Cheeky Wee Monkey: Puffins!

Why are budgies always so clever?
Cheeky Wee Monkey: Because they suck-seed!

Why did the goose cross the road?
Cheeky Wee Monkey: To prove he wasn't chicken!

What do Scottish owls sing?
Cheeky Wee Monkey: Owld Lang Syne!

BOW-WOW JOKES!

What goes woof, woof, tick, tock?
Cheeky Wee Monkey: A watchdog!

Why don't many blind people parachute?
Cheeky Wee Monkey: It can frighten the guide dog!

What animal always knows the time?
Cheeky Wee Monkey: A watch dog!

What's your dog's favourite food?
Cheeky Wee Monkey: Anything that's on my plate!

What did the dog say when he sat on sandpaper?
Cheeky Wee Monkey: Rough!

What do you get if you take a huge dog out for a walk?
Cheeky Wee Monkey: A Great Da-ne out!

Why must you be careful if it rains cats and dogs?
Cheeky Wee Monkey: You might step on a poodle!

What do you get if you cross a sheepdog with a daffodil?
Cheeky Wee Monkey: A collie-flower!

What is the only kind of dog you can eat?
Cheeky Wee Monkey: A hot dog!

What did the dog say when he bumped into a tree?
Cheeky Wee Monkey: Bark!

What kind of dog is always in a hurry?
Cheeky Wee Monkey: A dash-hound!

Why can't dogs dance very well?
Cheeky Wee Monkey: Because they have two left feet!

How do you stop a dog from barking in the back seat of a car?
Cheeky Wee Monkey: Pit it in the front seat!

What sometimes wears a coat in winter and pants in summer?
Cheeky Wee Monkey: A dog!

What do you get if you cross a snowman with a wolf?
Cheeky Wee Monkey: Frostbite!

How do you know if a dog is stupid?
Cheeky Wee Monkey: It chases parked cars!

NELLY THE ELEPHANT JOKES

How do you get six elephants into a matchbox?
Cheeky Wee Monkey: Take all the matches out first!

Why did the elephant eat the candle?
Cheeky Wee Monkey: It wanted a light snack!

Why can't you have two elephants in a swimming pool at the same time?
Cheeky Wee Monkey: They only have one set of trunks!

What's as big as an elephant but weighs nothing?
Cheeky Wee Monkey: The elephant's shadow!

What do you call an elephant that flies?
Cheeky Wee Monkey: A jumbo jet!

What's big, grey and wrinkly and jumps every minute?
Cheeky Wee Monkey: An elephant with hiccups!

What weighs five tons and is bright red?
Cheeky Wee Monkey: An elephant holding its breath!

What goes up very slowly but comes down very fast?
Cheeky Wee Monkey: An elephant in a lift!

What do you get if you cross a dog with an elephant?
Cheeky Wee Monkey: A very nervous postman!

What's grey, carries a box of chocolates and cheers you up when you are ill?
Cheeky Wee Monkey: A get wellephant!

How do you know that there's an elephant in your fridge?
Cheeky Wee Monkey: You cannae get the door closed!

What do you call someone with an elephant sitting on them?
Cheeky Wee Monkey: Squashed!

What did the hotel manager say to the elephant who wouldn't pay his bill?
Cheeky Wee Monkey: Pack up your trunk and go!

What do you give an elephant who is nervous?
Cheeky Wee Monkey: Trunkquilizers!

What do you call four elephants riding a bicycle?
Cheeky Wee Monkey: Optimistic!

What do you get if you cross a mole with an elephant?
Cheeky Wee Monkey: Lots of big holes in your garden!

How do you know there's an elephant under your bed?
Cheeky Wee Monkey: Your head touches the ceiling!

Where do elephants carry their luggage?
Cheeky Wee Monkey: In their trunks!

What's grey, huge and has sixteen wheels?
Cheeky Wee Monkey: An elephant on roller skates!

What time is it if an elephant sits on your garden fence?
Cheeky Wee Monkey: Time to get a new fence!

What should you do if you find an elephant in your bed?
Cheeky Wee Monkey: Find somewhere else tae sleep!

FISHY JOKES

Why was Isabella not frightened of the shark?
Cheeky Wee Monkey: It wis a man-eating shark!

What do sea monsters eat?
Cheeky Wee Monkey: Fish and ships!

Why did the whale cross the beach?
Cheeky Wee Monkey: To get to the other tide!

Why are some fish found at the bottom of the North Sea?
Cheeky Wee Monkey: Because they dropped out of a school!

How do fish know when they need to diet?
Cheeky Wee Monkey: They weigh themselves on their scales!

What kind of fish can't swim?
Cheeky Wee Monkey: Dead ones!

What did the boy octopus sing to the girl octopus?
Cheeky Wee Monkey: I wanna hold your hand, hand, hand, hand, hand!

What is an octopus?
Cheeky Wee Monkey: An eight-sided cat!

What do you do with a blue whale?
Cheeky Wee Monkey: Cheer it up!

What happened at Moby Dick's birthday party?
Cheeky Wee Monkey: They all had a whale of a time!

What happened when the fish had a fight with the chip?
Cheeky Wee Monkey: The fish got battered!

What's the difference between a piano and a fish?
Cheeky Wee Monkey: You can't tuna fish!

Why do fish live in salt water?
Cheeky Wee Monkey: Because pepper makes them sneeze!

How do you send a message to a salmon?
Cheeky Wee Monkey: Drop it a line!

What creatures stick to ships carrying sheep?
Cheeky Wee Monkey: Baaa-rnacles!

Where do fish sit on dining room tables?
Cheeky Wee Monkey: On plaice mats!

Why do dolphins never do anything by accident?
Cheeky Wee Monkey: Because they always do them on porpoise!

Why didn't Noah do much fishing?
Cheeky Wee Monkey: He only had two worms on the ark!

CREEPY-CRAWLIE JOKES

Where can you find giant snails?
Cheeky Wee Monkey: At the end of a giant's fingers!

What's Scottish, tiny but highly dangerous?
Cheeky Wee Monkey: A midge with a machine gun!

What do worms leave round their baths?
Cheeky Wee Monkey: The scum of the earth!

How can you tell which end of a worm is which?
Cheeky Wee Monkey: Tell it one of my jokes and see which end laughs!

What reads under your garden?
Cheeky Wee Monkey: Bookworms!

How do bees get to school?
Cheeky Wee Monkey: On the school buzz!

What's the difference between a bird and a fly?
Cheeky Wee Monkey: A bird can fly, but a fly can't bird!

Why was the mummy glow-worm unhappy?
Cheeky Wee Monkey: Because her children weren't very bright!

What did one bee say to the other on a warm day in Scotland?
Cheeky Wee Monkey: 'Swarm here, sure it is?

Where do fleas go in the winter?
Cheeky Wee Monkey: Search me!

What do large bees chew?
Cheeky Wee Monkey: Bumble gum!

How do you make a glow worm happy?
Cheeky Wee Monkey: Cut aff its tail. It'll be delighted!

What do you get if you cross a spider with an elephant?
Cheeky Wee Monkey: Well, if it walks across your ceiling, watch out!

What goes zzub, zzub?
Cheeky Wee Monkey: A bee flying backwards!

Cheeky Wee Monkey: Ah know a good insect joke.
What is it?
Cheeky Wee Monkey: Ah cannae remember and it's really bugging me!

What sort of insect is a slug?
Cheeky Wee Monkey: A homeless snail!

If two silk worms had a race, what would be the result?
Cheeky Wee Monkey: A tie!

Why do spiders like cars?
Cheeky Wee Monkey: So they can take them out for spins!

What is smaller than an ant's mouth?
Cheeky Wee Monkey: What it eats!

What's a midge's favourite pop star?
Cheeky Wee Monkey: Sting!

What's the difference between a dog and a flea?
Cheeky Wee Monkey: A dog can have fleas but a flea cannae have dogs?

What was the snail doing on the M8 motorway between Edinburgh and Glasgow?
Cheeky Wee Monkey: About two miles a year!

What do you get if you cross an insect with reindeer horns?
Cheeky Wee Monkey: Antlers!

Where did the vet take the sick wasp?
Cheeky Wee Monkey: To the waspital!

KRAZY ANIMAL QUACKER JOKES

What has two humps and is found at the top of Ben Nevis?
Cheeky Wee Monkey: A lost camel!

What do you call a cow eating grass in a field?
Cheeky Wee Monkey: A lawn mooer!

Why did the chicken cross the road, roll in mud, and then cross the road again?
Cheeky Wee Monkey: He wis a dirty double-crosser!

When is a cow not a cow?
Cheeky Wee Monkey: When it turns into a field!

Where in America do cows go on holiday?
Cheeky Wee Monkey: Moo York!

Can I feed the lions in Edinburgh zoo?
Cheeky Wee Monkey: No, but you can throw in money. The notice says, 'Do not feed. £50 fine.'

Why do white sheep eat more grass than black sheep?
Cheeky Wee Monkey: Because there's more of them!

Why did the dinosaur cross the road?
Cheeky Wee Monkey: Because chicken hadn't been invented!

Where do rabbits learn to fly?
Cheeky Wee Monkey: In the hare force!

Why did the lion eat the tightrope walker?
Cheeky Wee Monkey: It wanted a well-balanced meal!

What do you get if you cross a chicken with cement?
Cheeky Wee Monkey: A bricklayer!

Why do leopards never take a bath?
Cheeky Wee Monkey: They don't want to get spotlessly clean!

What is a prehistoric animal when it's asleep?
Cheeky Wee Monkey: A dinosnore!

What do tigers say before they start to hunt?
Cheeky Wee Monkey: Let us prey!

Why did the Shetland pony go to the doctor?
Cheeky Wee Monkey: It felt a little horse!

When does a cart come before a horse?
Cheeky Wee Monkey: In the dictionary!

What did the 18 stone mouse say?
Cheeky Wee Monkey: Here, kitty, kitty, kitty!

What do mummy cows sing when their calf has a birthday?
Cheeky Wee Monkey: Happy birthday to moo!

How do hedgehogs play at leapfrog?
Cheeky Wee Monkey: Very, very carefully!

Why can't leopards escape from zoos?
Cheeky Wee Monkey: Because they're always spotted!

What flowers do squirrels give on Valentine's Day?
Cheeky Wee Monkey: Forget-me-nuts!

Why are dinosaurs healthier then dragons?
Cheeky Wee Monkey: Because dinosaurs don't smoke!

What do you get if you cross a pig with a young goat?
Cheeky Wee Monkey: A dirty wee kid!

What do you get if you cross a dinosaur with a pig?
Cheeky Wee Monkey: Jurassic pork!

What do you call a cat that sucks lemons?
Cheeky Wee Monkey: A sour puss!

What do you call a bear with no socks on?
Cheeky Wee Monkey: A bare foot!

Why are there no giraffes in primary schools?
Cheeky Wee Monkey: Because they're all in high schools!

What's a frog's favourite opera?
Cheeky Wee Monkey: Swamp Lake!

What do hedgehogs say after they kiss?
Cheeky Wee Monkey: Ouch! That wis sore.

What did the stupid zookeeper call the zebra?
Cheeky Wee Monkey: Spot!

What did the mummy kangaroo say to the daddy kangaroo?
Cheeky Wee Monkey: Ah hate it when it's raining and the kids have to play inside!

What jumps up and down in front of a car on misty nights?
Cheeky Wee Monkey: Froglights!

Do crazy skunks celebrate Valentine's Day?
Cheeky Wee Monkey: Of course. Sure they're sent-imental!

Why did the cow cross the road?
Cheeky Wee Monkey: To get to the udder side!

What did the skunk say when the wind changed direction?
Cheeky Wee Monkey: It's all coming back to me now!

Why did the hedgehog cross the road?
Cheeky Wee Monkey: To see his flat mate!

Where do bulls get their messages?
Cheeky Wee Monkey: On a bull-etin board!

Did you hear about the nearsighted porcupine?
Cheeky Wee Monkey: Aye, it fell in love with a pincushion!

What kind of bunny drinks tea?
Cheeky Wee Monkey: Mugs Bunny!

Excuse me, I'm looking for a cat with one eye.
Cheeky Wee Monkey: Would you not be better using both eyes?

What do you call a bunch of rabbits all in a row, and moving backwards?
Cheeky Wee Monkey: A receding hare-line! (Ask dad if you don't get it!)

How do you know that carrots are good for eyesight?
Cheeky Wee Monkey: Have you ever seen a rabbit wearing glasses?

Why did the wee boy have dirt on his face?
Cheeky Wee Monkey: Because he had a mole on his cheek!

What do you call a blind dinosaur?
Cheeky Wee Monkey: A do-you-think-he-saur-us?

What do you call a donkey with only three legs?
Cheeky Wee Monkey: Wonkey!

What happened when the lion ate the dictionary?
Cheeky Wee Monkey: Nothing. He didn't breathe a word of it!

What happens if a frog breaks down?
Cheeky Wee Monkey: It gets toad away!

What do you call a disguise worn by an elk?
Cheeky Wee Monkey: A false moosetache!

What do Christmas and a cat walking on sand have in common?
Cheeky Wee Monkey: Sandy Claus!

Who invented the tunnel?
Cheeky Wee Monkey: A mole!

What did one pig email to the other?
Cheeky Wee Monkey: Let's be pen pals!

What kind of car does Mickey Mouse's wife drive?
Cheeky Wee Monkey: A Minnie!

What do cats eat for breakfast?
Cheeky Wee Monkey: Mice Krispies!

Why did the sheep say 'moo'?
Cheeky Wee Monkey: It wis learning another language!

What do you call a horse that lives next door?
Cheeky Wee Monkey: A neigh-bour!

What do cats sleep on?
Cheeky Wee Monkey: Catterpillows!

Why are there so many crabs in jail?
Cheeky Wee Monkey: They keep pinching things!

How did the lion feel after he was run over by a car?
Cheeky Wee Monkey: Tyred!

How do you attract a squirrel down from a tree?
Cheeky Wee Monkey: Act like a nutter!

What did the horse say when it fell?
Cheeky Wee Monkey: I've fallen and I can't giddyup!

What is the difference between a sick lion and seven days?
Cheeky Wee Monkey: One is a weak one and the other one week!

What did the daddy buffalo say to his wee boy before he went off on a trip?
Cheeky Wee Monkey: Bison!

Which cat makes the worst pet?
Cheeky Wee Monkey: A cat-astrophe!

What kind of money do polar bears use?
Cheeky Wee Monkey: Ice lolly!

Why did the lion wear trainers?
Cheeky Wee Monkey: His shoes were at the cobblers!

What did the sheep say to its mummy?
Cheeky Wee Monkey: Ah love ewe!

A man rode into town on Monday. The next day he rode back on Monday. How is this possible?
Cheeky Wee Monkey: The horse's name was Monday!

What do you get if you cross a skunk with a bear?
Cheeky Wee Monkey: Winnie the Pooh!

Why did the chicken not cross the road?
Cheeky Wee Monkey: Because there was a KFC on the other side!

Why do dragons sleep during the day?
Cheeky Wee Monkey: So they can fight knights!

What other animal do you almost look like when you are having a bath?
Cheeky Wee Monkey: A bit bear!

What pet makes the loudest noise?
Cheeky Wee Monkey: A trum-pet!

What's a mouse's favourite game?
Cheeky Wee Monkey: Hide and Squeak!

What do you get if you cross a grizzly bear with a harp?
Cheeky Wee Monkey: A bare-faced lyre!

What animal is always wet?
Cheeky Wee Monkey: A reindeer!

Why didn't the wee boy believe the tiger?
Cheeky Wee Monkey: He thought it was lion!

What's the difference between a lion and a biscuit?
Cheeky Wee Monkey: You cannae dunk a lion in yer tea!

What do you get if you cross a skunk with a boomerang?
Cheeky Wee Monkey: A smell you cannae get rid of!

Why can't a leopard hide?
Cheeky Wee Monkey: Because he's always spotted!

What ballet do squirrels like best?
Cheeky Wee Monkey: The Nutcracker!

What does a bear put in his house?
Cheeky Wee Monkey: Fur-niture!

Two monkeys were getting in a bath. One said, 'Ah, ah, ah, ah.' What did the other one say?
Cheeky Wee Monkey: Put some more cold water in!

What do you call a hairy beast with clothes on?
Cheeky Wee Monkey: A wear-wolf!

Why do some cows wear bells?
Cheeky Wee Monkey: Because their horns don't work!

Why did the chicken sit on the egg?
Cheeky Wee Monkey: It didn't have a chair!

What do you call a bald bear?
Cheeky Wee Monkey: Fred bare!

What did Goldilocks say when the three bears wanted to sit down?
Cheeky Wee Monkey: Three chairs for the three bears!

What do you get if you cross Bambi with a ghost?
Cheeky Wee Monkey: Bam-boo!

What nationality are hamsters?
Cheeky Wee Monkey: Dutch. They come from Hamsterdam!

When is a well-dressed lion like a weed?
Cheeky Wee Monkey: When he's a dandelion!

Why do giraffes have very long necks?
Cheeky Wee Monkey: Because their feet are so smelly!

How many skunks does it take to make a stink?
Cheeky Wee Monkey: Quite a phew!

What do you get when you cross a pie with a snake?
Cheeky Wee Monkey: A pie-thon!

What steps must you take when a lion is chasing you?
Cheeky Wee Monkey: Big ones!

What goes 'oo, oo, oo'?
Cheeky Wee Monkey: A cow with no lips!

What followed the dinosaur?
Cheeky Wee Monkey: It's tail!

What do you call a hungry horse in four letters?
Cheeky Wee Monkey: M.T.G.G.!

Why did the snake cross the road?
Cheeky Wee Monkey: To get to the other sssssssssside!

What do you call a bull that sleeps a lot?
Cheeky Wee Monkey: A bulldozer!

What did the judge say when the pig came into the courtroom?
Cheeky Wee Monkey: Odour in court!

What animal is 'out of bounds'?
Cheeky Wee Monkey: An exhausted kangaroo!

What's black and white and goes round and round?
Cheeky Wee Monkey: A zebra stuck in a revolving door!

How do you fit more pigs into a farm?
Cheeky Wee Monkey: Build a sty-scraper!

What do you get if you cross a mouse with a haggis?
Cheeky Wee Monkey: An offal wee sleekit courin' timorous beastie!

What kind of horses go out in the dark?
Cheeky Wee Monkey: Nightmares!

Where do sheep go for haircuts?
Cheeky Wee Monkey: To the ba ba shop!

What do you call a girl with a frog on her head?
Cheeky Wee Monkey: Lily!

OH, DOCTOR, DOCTOR!

Oh, doctor, doctor, I keep thinking I'm the Forth Bridge. What's come over me?
Doctor Cheeky Wee Monkey: Probably thousands of cars and trucks!

Oh, doctor, doctor, I feel awful. Will I tell you about the symptoms?
Doctor Cheeky Wee Monkey: No, I know about them. They're a cartoon family with a son called Bart!

Oh, doctor, doctor, I think I'm chocolate biscuits.
Doctor Cheeky Wee Monkey: Don't be silly. You're not chocolate biscuits. You're crackers!

Oh, doctor, doctor, I've got bad teeth, dreadful breath and smelly feet.
Doctor Cheeky Wee Monkey: Sounds like you've got Foot and Mouth disease!

Oh, doctor, doctor, I've swallowed a bullet.
Doctor Cheeky Wee Monkey: Well don't point yourself at me!

Oh, doctor, doctor, I snore so loudly I keep waking myself up.
Doctor Cheeky Wee Monkey: Try sleeping in another room!

Oh, doctor, doctor, I've swallowed a pen. What should I do?
Doctor Cheeky Wee Monkey: Use a pencil!

Oh, doctor, doctor, I've got trouble with my breathing.
Doctor Cheeky Wee Monkey: Don't worry. I'll give you something that will soon put a stop to that!

Oh, doctor, doctor, I keep thinking I'm a moth.
Doctor Cheeky Wee Monkey: Please get out of my light!

Oh, doctor, doctor, there's a raspberry growing out of my ear.
Doctor Cheeky Wee Monkey: I'll give you some cream to put on it!

Oh, doctor, doctor, I feel as if I have an insect crawling and biting all over me.
Doctor Cheeky Wee Monkey: Don't worry. There's a nasty bug going round at present!

Oh, doctor, doctor, I feel I am getting smaller.
Doctor Cheeky Wee Monkey: Well, you'll just have to be a little patient!

Oh, doctor, doctor, everyone thinks I tell lies.
Doctor Cheeky Wee Monkey: I can't believe that!

Oh, doctor, doctor, I can't get to sleep.
Doctor Cheeky Wee Monkey: Well, lie on the top of your telly and you'll soon drop off!

Oh, doctor, doctor, I feel like a spoon.
Doctor Cheeky Wee Monkey: Well just sit there and don't stir!

Oh, doctor, doctor, what can you give me for flat feet?
Doctor Cheeky Wee Monkey: A bicycle pump!

Oh, doctor, doctor, I've got a problem with my waterworks.
Doctor Cheeky Wee Monkey: Hold on and I'll give you the phone number of a good plumber!

Oh, doctor, doctor, I've got terrible wind.
Doctor Cheeky Wee Monkey: Have you tried a kite?

Oh, doctor, doctor, I've got a sore leg. What can I do?
Doctor Cheeky Wee Monkey: Try limping!

Oh, doctor, doctor, will this ointment you gave me clear up my spots?
Doctor Cheeky Wee Monkey: I never make rash promises!

Oh, doctor, doctor, my nose is always running.
Doctor Cheeky Wee Monkey: Well, stick out your foot and trip it up!

Oh, doctor, doctor, if I take these blue pills you've given me will I get better?
Doctor Cheeky Wee Monkey: Well, none of the patients I've given them to have ever come back to complain!

Oh, doctor, doctor, people keep telling me I'm a wheelbarrow.
Doctor Cheeky Wee Monkey: Just don't let them push you around!

Oh, doctor, doctor, I keep thinking I'm a bee.
Doctor Cheeky Wee Monkey: Oh, buzz off!

Oh, doctor, doctor, I'm a burglar.
Doctor Cheeky Wee Monkey: Have you taken anything?

Oh, doctor, doctor, my arm is sore when I lift it up.
Doctor Cheeky Wee Monkey: Well, don't lift it up!

Oh, doctor, doctor, you must help me out.
Doctor Cheeky Wee Monkey: Just take the door on your left!

Oh, doctor, doctor, my baby is the image of my old auntie.
Doctor Cheeky Wee Monkey: Never mind. As long as he's healthy.

Oh, doctor, doctor, I've only got fifty seconds to live.
Doctor Cheeky Wee Monkey: Hold on a minute, please!

Oh, doctor, doctor, I keep thinking I'm a clock.
Doctor Cheeky Wee Monkey: Relax. Don't get yourself all wound up!

Oh, doctor, doctor, I think I'm a vampire.
Doctor Cheeky Wee Monkey: Necks please!

Oh, doctor, doctor, I've had my appendix out, my tonsils, my adenoids, my varicose veins, my gall bladder and all my teeth.
Doctor Cheeky Wee Monkey: Now, that's quite enough out of you!

Oh, doctor, doctor, everyone thinks I'm a bore.
Doctor Cheeky Wee Monkey: Just keep talking and I'll have a wee nap!

Oh, doctor, doctor, I feel like a greyhound.
Doctor Cheeky Wee Monkey: Take one of these pills every three laps!

Oh, doctor, doctor, I keep thinking I'm a nit.
Doctor Cheeky Wee Monkey: Will you please get out of my hair!

Oh, doctor, doctor, I feel like an elastic band.
Doctor Cheeky Wee Monkey: Come on. That's stretching it a bit far!

Oh, doctor, doctor, I think I'm a snail.
Doctor Cheeky Wee Monkey: Don't worry, we'll soon bring you out of your shell!

Oh, doctor, doctor, what did the x-ray of my brain show?
Doctor Cheeky Wee Monkey: Nothing whatsoever!

Oh, doctor, doctor, I feel like a sheep.
Doctor Cheeky Wee Monkey: That sounds very baaaaaaaaad!

Oh, doctor, doctor, I think I have magical powers.
Doctor Cheeky Wee Monkey: Well, you had better lie down for a spell!

Oh, doctor, doctor, I keep thinking I'm a caterpillar.
Doctor Cheeky Wee Monkey: Don't worry, you'll soon change!

Oh, doctor, doctor, I keep painting myself gold.
Doctor Cheeky Wee Monkey: It's probably a gilt complex!

Oh, doctor, doctor, I can't pronounce my Fs, Ts or Hs.
Doctor Cheeky Wee Monkey: Well, you can't say fairer than that!

Oh, doctor, doctor, the ointment you gave me is making my hands smart.
Doctor Cheeky Wee Monkey: Well, rub some on your head!

Oh, doctor, doctor, I have bananas growing out of my ears.
Doctor Cheeky Wee Monkey: Great! I love bananas.

Oh, doctor, doctor, I keep thinking I'm a spider.
Doctor Cheeky Wee Monkey: Don't spin your web of lies to me!

Oh, doctor, doctor, I keep thinking I'm an apple.
Doctor Cheeky Wee Monkey: We must get to the core of this!

Oh, doctor, doctor, I've just swallowed my mouth organ.
Doctor Cheeky Wee Monkey: Well, thank goodness you weren't playing a trumpet!

Oh, doctor, doctor, my entire left side is missing.
Doctor Cheeky Wee Monkey: Well at least you're all right now!

Oh, doctor, doctor, I feel like a drawing pin.
Doctor Cheeky Wee Monkey: Well, I can see your point.

Oh, doctor, doctor, I keep thinking I'm a mosquito.
Doctor Cheeky Wee Monkey: Hi, sucker!

Oh, doctor, doctor, I feel like a chocolate.
Doctor Cheeky Wee Monkey: So do I. Have you got any on you?

Oh, doctor, doctor, I feel like an apple.
Doctor Cheeky Wee Monkey: Don't worry, I'm not going to bite you!

Oh, doctor, doctor, I think I'm a bell.
Doctor Cheeky Wee Monkey: Take these pills and if they don't help give me a ring!

Oh, doctor, doctor, I keep thinking I'm a frog.
Doctor Cheeky Wee Monkey: Well don't croak on me!

Oh, doctor, doctor, I'm becoming invisible.
Doctor Cheeky Wee Monkey: Yes, I can see you're not all there!

Oh, doctor, doctor, I think I'm invisible.
Doctor Cheeky Wee Monkey: Who said that?

Oh, doctor, doctor, I feel like a pair of curtains.
Doctor Cheeky Wee Monkey: For goodness sake pull yourself together!

Oh, doctor, doctor, there's a fishy smell from my feet.
Doctor Cheeky Wee Monkey: You poor sole!

Oh, doctor, doctor, I think I'm a dog.
Doctor Cheeky Wee Monkey: Sit!

Oh, doctor, doctor, I'm boiling.
Doctor Cheeky Wee Monkey: Now, simmer down!

Oh, doctor, doctor, a grape seed has gone down the wrong way.
Doctor Cheeky Wee Monkey: Don't worry, you'll be vine soon!

Oh, doctor, doctor, why do you want me to stick out my tongue when the nurse examines me?
Doctor Cheeky Wee Monkey: Because I don't like her!

Oh, doctor, doctor, I get a terrible pain in my eye when I drink a cup of tea.
Doctor Cheeky Wee Monkey: Try taking the spoon out of the cup!

Oh, doctor, doctor, I've swallowed a fish bone and I'm choking.
Doctor Cheeky Wee Monkey: Well stop joking and tell me what's wrong with you!

Oh, doctor, doctor, some days I feel like a wigwam and other days like a tepee.
Doctor Cheeky Wee Monkey: The problem is you are too tense.

Oh, doctor, doctor, I feel like a pack of cards.
Doctor Cheeky Wee Monkey: I'll deal with you in a minute!

Oh, doctor, doctor, I think I'm a butterfly.
Doctor Cheeky Wee Monkey: Please say what you really mean and stop fluttering about!

Oh, doctor, doctor, my breathing is coming in short pants.
Doctor Cheeky Wee Monkey: It should be coming out of your lungs!

Oh, doctor, doctor, my breathing is still coming in short pants.
Doctor Cheeky Wee Monkey: It's a cold day. You should be wearing long trousers!

Oh, doctor, doctor, I think I'm a shepherd.
Doctor Cheeky Wee Monkey: I wouldn't lose any sheep over that!

Oh, doctor, doctor, I feel like an electric plug.
Doctor Cheeky Wee Monkey: That's shocking!

Oh, doctor, doctor, I keep thinking I'm a hundred pound note.
Doctor Cheeky Wee Monkey: Well, go on a holiday. The change will do you good.

WEE SMASHERS!

Cheeky Wee Monkey: Dae ye know the silly person who goes around saying 'no'?
No.
Cheeky Wee Monkey: Oh, so it's you!

What is white when dirty and black when clean?
Cheeky Wee Monkey: A blackboard!

What's green, huffy and got lots of muscles?
Cheeky Wee Monkey: The Incredible Sulk!

What month has 28 days?
Cheeky Wee Monkey: They all have!

What kind of bed does a mermaid sleep in?
Cheeky Wee Monkey: A waterbed!

Who makes suits and eats spinach?
Cheeky Wee Monkey: Popeye the tailorman!

Why did the boy become an alien?
Cheeky Wee Monkey: Because he wis no earthly good!

Why did the musician keep his trumpet in the fridge?
Cheeky Wee Monkey: He liked to play cool music!

What is the fruitiest school lesson?
Cheeky Wee Monkey: History, because it's full of dates!

What did the lady railway employee wear on her feet?
Cheeky Wee Monkey: Platform shoes!

What did the hat say to the scarf?
Cheeky Wee Monkey: You hang around and ah'll go on ahead!

Why did the customer in the hairdressers win the race?
Cheeky Wee Monkey: He was given a short cut!

What's yellow, brown and hairy?
Cheeky Wee Monkey: Cheese on toast that falls on the carpet!

Why were the nose and the handkerchief always fighting?
Cheeky Wee Monkey: Every time they met they came to blows!

What illness did everyone on the Enterprise catch?
Cheeky Wee Monkey: Chicken Spocks!

What did the one eye say to the other eye?
Cheeky Wee Monkey: Between you and me, something smells!

How do you get two pipers to play in perfect harmony?
Cheeky Wee Monkey: Shoot one!

How do you stop a cold going into your chest?
Cheeky Wee Monkey: Tie a knot in your neck!

What do poor people have, rich people don't have, and if you eat it you die?
Cheeky Wee Monkey: Nothing!

Which nursery rhyme character lives in Scotland?
Cheeky Wee Monkey: Little Miss Moffat!

What is hail?
Cheeky Wee Monkey: Hard-boiled rain!

Who is the boss of the hankies?
Cheeky Wee Monkey: The hankie-chief!

If 2 is company but 3 is a crowd, what are 4 and 5?
Cheeky Wee Monkey: 9!

Who is a snowman's favourite aunt?
Cheeky Wee Monkey: Aunt Artica!

Which Scottish Island is always thinking?
Cheeky Wee Monkey: Mull. It always likes tae mull things over!

What do spiders do on computers?
Cheeky Wee Monkey: Make web-sites!

Why did the computer get glasses?
Cheeky Wee Monkey: To improve its web-sight!

Why did the computer sneeze?
Cheeky Wee Monkey: It had a virus!

What did one shoelace say to the other shoelace?
Cheeky Wee Monkey: That's knot mine!

How does an Eskimo build his house?
Cheeky Wee Monkey: Igloos it together!

Why did the girl throw the clock out of the window?
Cheeky Wee Monkey: Because she wanted tae see time fly!

What did the mummy brush say to the baby brush?
Cheeky Wee Monkey: Go tae sweep!

What do you get if you cross very loud music with an English teacher?
Cheeky Wee Monkey: Punctuation!

What stays in the corner yet travels all over the world?
Cheeky Wee Monkey: A stamp!

Why are astronauts so successful?
Cheeky Wee Monkey: Because they always go up in the world.

What did the Scottish sailor who lived on an island say?
Cheeky Wee Monkey: Iona wee boat!

Why can only tiny fairies sit under toadstools?
Cheeky Wee Monkey: Because there's not mushroom!

Why are chefs cruel?
Cheeky Wee Monkey: Because they whip cream an' beat eggs!

What do you call a boy who rolls in leaves?
Cheeky Wee Monkey: Russell!

Why are Egyptians often confused?
Cheeky Wee Monkey: Because sometimes their daddies can be mummies!

Which four days of the week start with 'T'?
Cheeky Wee Monkey: Tuesday, Thursday, today and tomorrow!

Why were the giant's fingers only eleven inches long?
Cheeky Wee Monkey: Because if they were twelve inches they'd have been a foot!

Why did the window go to the doctor?
Cheeky Wee Monkey: He was havin' window panes!

What did one tooth say to the other tooth?
Cheeky Wee Monkey: I've got a date. The dentist is going to take me out!

What did the fireman's wife get for Christmas?
Cheeky Wee Monkey: A ladder in her stocking!

Why have you got all that rubbish on your bike?
Cheeky Wee Monkey: Ah'm recycling it!

Why was the doctor frustrated?
Cheeky Wee Monkey: Because he had nae patients!

What do you use to fix a broken tooth?
Cheeky Wee Monkey: Toothpaste!

What is the hardest bit about parachuting?
Cheeky Wee Monkey: The ground!

Did you hear about the robbery at the laundry yesterday?
Cheeky Wee Monkey: Aye, four clothes-pegs held up two shirts!

Why did the jelly wobble?
Cheeky Wee Monkey: Because it saw the milk shake!

What did the envelope say to the stamp?
Cheeky Wee Monkey: Stick wi' me and we can go places!

Where do they sell thick chips in Scotland?
Cheeky Wee Monkey: Dum-fries!

What's an eight letter word that only has one letter in it?
Cheeky Wee Monkey: Envelope!

Rain falls, but does it ever rise again?
Cheeky Wee Monkey: Aye, in dew time!

Which is heavier, a full moon or a half moon?
Cheeky Wee Monkey: The half moon because the full moon is lighter!

What runs but can't walk?
Cheeky Wee Monkey: The tap!

What is a tornado?
Cheeky Wee Monkey: Mother Nature daein' the twist!

Which is heaviest, a ton of feathers or a ton of bricks?
Cheeky Wee Monkey: They both weigh the same . . . a ton!

What is black and white and red all over?
Cheeky Wee Monkey: A newspaper!

How do you make anti-freeze?
Cheeky Wee Monkey: Steal her duvet!

What has one head, one foot and four legs?
Cheeky Wee Monkey: A bed!

What month do Scottish soldiers hate most?
Cheeky Wee Monkey: March!

How do you clean a trumpet?
Cheeky Wee Monkey: With a tuba toothpaste!

How can you tell if someone is changing into a fridge?
Cheeky Wee Monkey: A wee light comes on when they open their mouth!

Why did the burglar take a bath?
Cheeky Wee Monkey: He wanted tae make a clean getaway!

What did the grape do when it got stepped on?
Cheeky Wee Monkey: It let oot a little wine!

If you are on a trampoline what season of the year is it?
Cheeky Wee Monkey: Spring time!

What has teeth but cannot eat?
Cheeky Wee Monkey: A comb!

What can you serve but never eat?
Cheeky Wee Monkey: A tennis ball!

If a Red Indian's wife is called a squaw, what are Red Indian babies called?
Cheeky Wee Monkey: Squawkers!

Are you saving up for a rainy day?
Cheeky Wee Monkey: Aye, so far I've got an umbrella, wellingtons and a canoe!

What do you call a judge with no thumbs?
Cheeky Wee Monkey: Just his fingers!

Did you hear the joke about a roof?
Cheeky Wee Monkey: Never mind, it's probably o'er your heid!

Why was 6 afraid of 7?
Cheeky Wee Monkey: Because 789!

Cheeky Wee Monkey: Did ye ever hear the rope joke?
No.
Cheeky Wee Monkey: Och, skip it!

Why did the girl sprinkle sugar on her pillow?
Cheeky Wee Monkey: Because she liked sweet dreams!

Why is perfume obedient?
Cheeky Wee Monkey: Because it goes where it's scent.

How do you cure a headache?
Cheeky Wee Monkey: Jist put your head through a window and the pane will disappear!

Why did the rabbit cross the road?
Cheeky Wee Monkey: It was the chicken's day off!

What did the man from Mars say to the garden?
Cheeky Wee Monkey: Take me to yer weeder!

What kind of ticks do you find on the moon?
Cheeky Wee Monkey: Luna-ticks!

What kind of dream are you having when it is all about a man in a tin suit chasing you?
Cheeky Wee Monkey: A knightmare!

What do you call blind people with one leg and red hair who travel in trains?
Cheeky Wee Monkey: Passengers!

What's the difference between a teacher and a train?
Cheeky Wee Monkey: A teacher says 'spit yer chewing gum oot', and a train says 'chew chew'!

What do you call two people who always embarrass you in front of your friends?
Cheeky Wee Monkey: Mummy an' Daddy!

Why don't eggs tell jokes?
Cheeky Wee Monkey: They'd crack up at each other!

Where can you find an ocean with no water?
Cheeky Wee Monkey: On a map!

Why do cemeteries have walls round them?
Cheeky Wee Monkey: Because lots of folks are dying to get in!

Where did the musician leave his keys?
Cheeky Wee Monkey: In the piano!

What is the name of a girl with a sheep on her head?
Cheeky Wee Monkey: Baar-baa-ra!

What did one wall say to the other wall?
Cheeky Wee Monkey: Ah'll meet you at the corner!

What did the lumberjack say to his wife in December?
Cheeky Wee Monkey: Not many chopping days left till Christmas!

Why do the Scottish mountains never get cold in winter?
Cheeky Wee Monkey: They wear snow caps!

What did the digital watch say to the grandfather clock?
Cheeky Wee Monkey: Look Grandpa, no hands!

Why did the Queen go to the dentist?
Cheeky Wee Monkey: Tae have her teeth crowned!

What word is always pronounced wrongly?
Cheeky Wee Monkey: Wrongly!

What did Batman and Robin become when they were run over by a bus?
Cheeky Wee Monkey: Flatman and Ribbon!

What do you say when King Kong wins a prize?
Cheeky Wee Monkey: Kong-ratulations!

Why was the employee fired from the orange juice factory?
Cheeky Wee Monkey: He couldn't concentrate!

What goes through Glasgow, Edinburgh and Aberdeen but doesn't move?
Cheeky Wee Monkey: Roads!

Which bus has crossed the Atlantic Ocean?
Cheeky Wee Monkey: Columbus!

How does the man in the moon cut his hair?
Cheeky Wee Monkey: Eclipse it!

What kind of star is very dangerous?
Cheeky Wee Monkey: A shooting star!

What lies on its back a hundred feet in the air?
Cheeky Wee Monkey: A centipede!

What do you call a female magician?
Cheeky Wee Monkey: Trixie!

Why did the photograph go to jail?
Cheeky Wee Monkey: Because it wis framed!

What do you call the Loch Ness Monster with a whale in each ear?
Cheeky Wee Monkey: Anything you want. It cannae hear you!

What would you call the Loch Ness Monster if it ate everyone in Scotland?
Cheeky Wee Monkey: Lonely!

Why did the farmer plough his field with a steamroller?
Cheeky Wee Monkey: Because he was growing mashed potatoes!

What do you call insects in Gretna Green?
Cheeky Wee Monkey: Ant-elopes!

How did the dog get all his fleas?
Cheeky Wee Monkey: They're itch-hikers!

What do you call a lady with one leg?
Cheeky Wee Monkey: Eileen!

How did the baker mop up the spilt milk?
Cheeky Wee Monkey: He used a sponge cake!

How many chestnuts grow on a Scottish fir tree?
Cheeky Wee Monkey: None. They grow on horse-chestnut trees!

Did you pick your nose?
Cheeky Wee Monkey: No, I was born with it!

What is the difference between a Scottish mountain and a pill?
Cheeky Wee Monkey: One is hard to get up and one is hard to get down!

What is Cole's Law?
Cheeky Wee Monkey: It's sort of thinly sliced cabbage!

What's a hundred and fifty feet high, lives in Italy and is mostly made of dough?
Cheeky Wee Monkey: The Leaning Tower of Pizza!

Why did the wee boy throw his sandwich out of the window?
Cheeky Wee Monkey: He wanted to see the butter fly!

What happens when dog fleas get angry?
Cheeky Wee Monkey: They become hopping mad!

What do you get in December that you don't get in any other month?
Cheeky Wee Monkey: The letter 'D'!

What has two handles, is filled with food and lives in a bell tower?
Cheeky Wee Monkey: The lunch bag of Notre Dame!

Why did the tortoise cross the road?
Cheeky Wee Monkey: To get to the Shell station!

What has no beginning, no end, and nothing in the middle?
Cheeky Wee Monkey: A doughnut!

If the former ruler of Russia was called a Czar what were his children called?
Cheeky Wee Monkey: Czardines!

What do you call an unhappy spaceship?
Cheeky Wee Monkey: An unidentified crying object!

On which day do cannibals eat people?
Cheeky Wee Monkey: Chewsday!

What do you call a large fish that swims in Scottish lochs and has a motorbike?
Cheeky Wee Monkey: A motor pike!

What do you call an underground train full of MSPs?
Cheeky Wee Monkey: A tube who think they're Smarties!

What happened to the orange when he crossed the road?
Cheeky Wee Monkey: He became orange squash!

Who designed Noah's ark?
Cheeky Wee Monkey: An ark-itect!

What did one flea say to the other flea?
Cheeky Wee Monkey: Should we walk or take a dog?

Excuse me, but will this path take me to the main road?
Cheeky Wee Monkey: No, you'll need to go yourself!

Why did the fig go out with the prune?
Cheeky Wee Monkey: It couldnae find another date!

What do you get if you cross a jellyfish with a plane?
Cheeky Wee Monkey: A jelly-copter!

What goes mooz?
Cheeky Wee Monkey: A jet plane flying backwards!

What happens if two bedbugs fall in love?
Cheeky Wee Monkey: They probably get married in the spring!

What do elves learn in school?
Cheeky Wee Monkey: The elf-abet!

How do spacemen get their baby to sleep in its cot?
Cheeky Wee Monkey: They rocket!

Why are you covered in bruises?
Cheeky Wee Monkey: I started to walk through a revolving door and then changed my mind!

What name is given to most male camels?
Cheeky Wee Monkey: Humphrey!

What bow can't be tied?
Cheeky Wee Monkey: A rainbow!

Why do dustmen never accept any invitations?
Cheeky Wee Monkey: Because they're refuse men!

What did one pencil say to the other pencil?
Cheeky Wee Monkey: Yer looking awfa sharp today!

What do hippies do if they see a space-man?
Cheeky Wee Monkey: Park in it quick, man!

Why did the chewing gum cross the road?
Cheeky Wee Monkey: It was stuck to the chicken's foot!

What cheese is made backwards?
Cheeky Wee Monkey: Edam!

What stories do ships' captains tell their children?
Cheeky Wee Monkey: Ferry stories!

What did one star say to the other star?
Cheeky Wee Monkey: Nice to meteor!

What did the ground say to the earthquake?
Cheeky Wee Monkey: You really crack me up!

Which Star Wars villain wears a black helmet and goes 'quack quack'?
Cheeky Wee Monkey: Duck Vader!

Who is the king of the class?
Cheeky Wee Monkey: The ruler!

What do you call something that runs around a garden all day and never stops?
Cheeky Wee Monkey: A fence!

What do you call a man buried in the garden?
Cheeky Wee Monkey: Pete!

What happened to the man who sat on a tube of chocolate sweets?
Cheeky Wee Monkey: He became a right Smartie pants!

What does everyone overlook?
Cheeky Wee Monkey: Their nose!

What are the best days to go off in a spaceship?
Cheeky Wee Monkey: Moondays and Sundays!

Is that a wonder watch costing fifty pence you're wearing?
Cheeky Wee Monkey: Aye, every time I look at it I wonder if it's still working!

What did the carpet robber say to the floor?
Cheeky Wee Monkey: You go ahead, ah'll cover you!

What do you get if you cross a chicken with a zebra?
Cheeky Wee Monkey: A four-legged meal with its very own barcode.

THEY'LL DRIVE YOU BANANAS!

What has eyes but cannot see?
Cheeky Wee Monkey: A potato!

What has teeth but cannot eat?
Cheeky Wee Monkey: A comb!

What kind of ear does a ship have?
Cheeky Wee Monkey: An engineer!

What goes up but never comes down?
Cheeky Wee Monkey: Yer age!

What makes music on your head?
Cheeky Wee Monkey: A head band!

What do you call a Scotsman wearing a coat?
Cheeky Wee Monkey: Mac!

What do you call a Scotsman without a coat?
Cheeky Wee Monkey: Cold!

What do you get if you cross a planet with a silver cup?
Cheeky Wee Monkey: A constellation prize!

Where does success come before work?
Cheeky Wee Monkey: In the dictionary!

What do you get if you cross a crocodile, a gorilla and a parrot?
Cheeky Wee Monkey: I'm not sure, but if it talked I'd sure listen!

Did Mary Queen of Scots have a bad temper?
Cheeky Wee Monkey: Well, she certainly lost her head!

Why is it unsafe to sleep on trains?
Cheeky Wee Monkey: Because they run over sleepers!

Which is the fastest, cold or heat?
Cheeky Wee Monkey: Heat, because you can always catch a cold!

Who stole the soap?
Cheeky Wee Monkey: The robber duck!

What can you wear that never goes out of fashion?
Cheeky Wee Monkey: A smile!

How do we know that calendars are popular?
Cheeky Wee Monkey: Because they always have lots of dates!

What is smelly and round with peals of laughter?
Cheeky Wee Monkey: A tickled onion!

How do gardeners mend their trousers?
Cheeky Wee Monkey: With cabbage-patches!

What three things can you never have for breakfast?
Cheeky Wee Monkey: Lunch, dinner and supper!

What is a personal computer's favourite kind of dance?
Cheeky Wee Monkey: Disco dancing!

What did the sheet say to the bed?
Cheeky Wee Monkey: I've got you covered!

How do you start a teddy bear race?
Cheeky Wee Monkey: You say, ready, teddy, go!

Why can't a man living in Scotland be buried in England?
Cheeky Wee Monkey: Because he's still alive!

What is an archaeologist?
Cheeky Wee Monkey: Someone whose career is in ruins!

Why was the brush late?
Cheeky Wee Monkey: It over swept!

Who invented fractions?
Cheeky Wee Monkey: Henry the Eighth!

What's worse than finding a worm in your apple?
Cheeky Wee Monkey: Finding only half a worm!

What's your ambition in life, Cheeky Wee Monkey?
Cheeky Wee Monkey: Climb the Empire State Building like my old Uncle Kong!

What did the Sleeping Beauty say when she lost her camera?
Cheeky Wee Monkey: Some day my prints will come!

What do you call a Roman emperor with a cold?
Cheeky Wee Monkey: Julius Sneezer!

Why did the cannibal live on his own?
Cheeky Wee Monkey: He was fed up with other people!

What do you get if you cross a spaceship with a waitress?
Cheeky Wee Monkey: A flying saucer!

What gets wetter the more it dries?
Cheeky Wee Monkey: A towel!

Where did the cheeky mistletoe go to become a Member of the Scottish Parliament?
Cheeky Wee Monkey: Holly-rude.

What kind of keys scratch themselves under the arms?
Cheeky Wee Monkey: Monkeys!

Which hand is best to write with?
Cheeky Wee Monkey: Neither. It's best to write with a pen!

Which painting is forever complaining?
Cheeky Wee Monkey: The Moaning Lisa!

What do you call a man stuck in a post box?
Cheeky Wee Monkey: Bill!

What is the longest word?
Cheeky Wee Monkey: 'What' isn't the longest word. 'Smiles' is the longest word as there's a mile between each 'S'!

What's the height of stupidity?
Cheeky Wee Monkey: I don't know. How tall are you?

Who was the biggest robber in history?
Cheeky Wee Monkey: Atlas. He held up the whole world!

What goes up and down yet doesn't move?
Cheeky Wee Monkey: Stairs!

What do you say when you cross a mouse with a camera?
Cheeky Wee Monkey: Cheese!

What holds the moon in the sky?
Cheeky Wee Monkey: Moonbeams!

What do you call a toy railway?
Cheeky Wee Monkey: A Play Station!

What did the stamp say to the envelope?
Cheeky Wee Monkey: I'm stuck on you!

Which mountain is always on the go?
Cheeky Wee Monkey: Mount Never-rest!

If your auntie ran off to get married what would she be?
Cheeky Wee Monkey: An antelope!

What is the difference between here and there?
Cheeky Wee Monkey: The letter 't'!

What is the full name of a boy called Lee who no one talks to?
Cheeky Wee Monkey: Lone Lee!

A greengrocer is six feet six inches tall, wears size eleven shoes and is called Hamish. What does he weigh?
Cheeky Wee Monkey: Potatoes!

When I grow up I want to be a ballet dancer.
Cheeky Wee Monkey: Well. That'll keep you on your toes!

What invention allows people to see through walls?
Cheeky Wee Monkey: Windows!

What do you call a freight train carrying toffee?
Cheeky Wee Monkey: A chew chew!

Why did the boy pitch his tent on top of the cooker?
Cheeky Wee Monkey: Because he wanted a home on the range!

What do you call a man who thieves?
Cheeky Wee Monkey: Robin!

Why do you put soap bubbles in your ear?
Cheeky Wee Monkey: I like to hear all about soap operas!

What do you call a man trying to lift a car?
Cheeky Wee Monkey: Jack!

Why was the belt arrested?
Cheeky Wee Monkey: Because it held up some trousers!

Why is Scotland so wet?
Cheeky Wee Monkey: Because the Queen has reigned for over fifty years!

What is the only thing you break when you say its name?
Cheeky Wee Monkey: Silence!

Will an apple a day keep the doctor away?
Cheeky Wee Monkey: Only if your aim is good!

What do you call a man with a lot of debt?
Cheeky Wee Monkey: Owen!

How did the Vikings send messages to the Scots?
Cheeky Wee Monkey: By Norse code!

What did the judge say to the dentist?
Cheeky Wee Monkey: Dae ye swear to pull the tooth, the whole tooth an' nothin' but the tooth?

I know a magician who saws people in half.
Cheeky Wee Monkey: I bet he has lots of half-brothers and sisters!

Have you ever had any trouble with pneumonia?
Cheeky Wee Monkey: Only when I try to spell it!

Why is everyone in Scotland so tired on the 1st April?
Cheeky Wee Monkey: Because they have just finished a March of 31 days!

What do Robert the Bruce and Kermit the frog have in common?
Cheeky Wee Monkey: The same middle name!

What do you call an Egyptian Mummy that washes up?
Cheeky Wee Monkey: Pharaoh Liquid!

What is the laziest part of a car?
Cheeky Wee Monkey: The wheels, because they're always tired!

What's the first thing the Queen did when she ascended to the throne?
Cheeky Wee Monkey: Sat down!

How do you keep an idiot in suspense?
Cheeky Wee Monkey: I'll tell you tomorrow!

Why is the River Clyde so relaxed?
Cheeky Wee Monkey: Because it just goes with the flow!

Who is Peter Pan's smelly friend?
Cheeky Wee Monkey: Stinkerbell!

What is a moon man's favourite place on a personal computer?
Cheeky Wee Monkey: The space bar!

What do you call two banana skins?
Cheeky Wee Monkey: A pair o' slippers!

Have you heard the joke about butter?
Cheeky Wee Monkey: Ah better no' tell you. You might spread it!

Why did Henry the Eighth have so many wives?
Cheeky Wee Monkey: Maybe he liked to chop and change!

What do you call a royal person who has drawings of large fish?
Cheeky Wee Monkey: The Prints of Whales!

Why did the haggis cross the road?
Cheeky Wee Monkey: To escape from the Burns Supper!

Why did the boy run round his bed?
Cheeky Wee Monkey: To try to catch up on his sleep!

What kind of music are balloons frightened of?
Cheeky Wee Monkey: Pop!

What happens if you eat yeast and shoe polish?
Cheeky Wee Monkey: Every morning you'll rise and shine!

What do you call a month of rain in Scotland?
Cheeky Wee Monkey: Summer!

What do you call pubs on Mars?
Cheeky Wee Monkey: Mars bars!

Why was Edward's army too tired to fight at the Battle of Bannockburn?
Cheeky Wee Monkey: They had lots o' sleepless knights!

Where do moon people go after their marriage?
Cheeky Wee Monkey: On honeyearth!

Why don't traffic lights go swimming?
Cheeky Wee Monkey: Because they take a long time tae change!

Who made King Arthur's round table?
Cheeky Wee Monkey: Sir Cumference!

Why did the bacon laugh?
Cheeky Wee Monkey: Because the egg cracked a yolk!

Why did the cowboy take hay to bed?
Cheeky Wee Monkey: He wanted tae feed his nightmares!

What do astronauts eat at lunch?
Cheeky Wee Monkey: Whatever is in their launch boxes!

What has lots of faces and sings?
Cheeky Wee Monkey: A choir!

What has five eyes that are always wet?
Cheeky Wee Monkey: The Mississippi River!

Which Scot makes spaghetti?
Cheeky Wee Monkey: MacAronni!

What do you get if you cross a scary creature with a person who has a high IQ?
Cheeky Wee Monkey: Frank Einstein's monster!

Do you put on a clean pair of socks every day?
Cheeky Wee Monkey: Aye, but at the end o' the week ah cannae get ma feet intae ma shoes!

What do you call a man with a pig on his head?
Cheeky Wee Monkey: Hamlet!

Why are you eating your meal using a spade?
Cheeky Wee Monkey: Ah like tae shovel it down!

What did the paper clip say to the magnet?
Cheeky Wee Monkey: Oh, you're so attractive. I feel myself drawn to you!

What are all babies' mottos?
Cheeky Wee Monkey: If at first ye don't succeed, cry, cry again!

What happened to the dustman who complained he didn't have anywhere to put the rubbish?
Cheeky Wee Monkey: He got the sack!

What did the big phone say to the little phone?
Cheeky Wee Monkey: You're too young to be engaged!

Cheeky Wee Monkey: Ah just sat down on a pin.
Did it hurt?
Cheeky Wee Monkey: Naw, it was a safety pin!

What did one light bulb say to the other light bulb?
Cheeky Wee Monkey: I love you a whole watt!

Who makes suits and eats spinach?
Cheeky Wee Monkey: Popeye the tailorman!

What starts with a 'P', ends with an 'E', and has over a million letters in it?
Cheeky Wee Monkey: The Post Office!

Where do snowmen keep their money?
Cheeky Wee Monkey: In snow banks!

What did the pencil say to the paper?
Cheeky Wee Monkey: I dot my I's on you!

What do dentists call patients' X-rays.
Cheeky Wee Monkey: Tooth pics!

What did the caveman give his wife on Valentine's Day?
Cheeky Wee Monkey: Uughs and kisses!

What happened when the Highland dancer washed her kilt?
Cheeky Wee Monkey: She couldn't do a fling with it!

What did the raspberry syrup say to the ice cream?
Cheeky Wee Monkey: I'm sweet on you!

What did the painter say to the wall?
Cheeky Wee Monkey: Wan more crack and ah'll plaster you!

What was Humpty Dumpty wearing when he fell off the wall?
Cheeky Wee Monkey: A shellsuit.

What kind of lights did Noah have on the ark?
Cheeky Wee Monkey: Floodlights.

Why did the balloon burst?
Cheeky Wee Monkey: Because it saw the lolly pop!

Why did the personal computer squeak?
Cheeky Wee Monkey: Because someone stepped on its mouse!

What do you call a man with flowers and bushes on his head?
Cheeky Wee Monkey: Gordon!

What is the strongest vegetable in the world?
Cheeky Wee Monkey: Muscle sprout!

What's the best thing to put in a cake?
Cheeky Wee Monkey: Yer teeth!

What do you call a line of Barbie dolls?
Cheeky Wee Monkey: A barbeque!

Why did the banana cross the road?
Cheeky Wee Monkey: It a pealed tae him!

What did the pencil sharpener say to the pencil?
Cheeky Wee Monkey: Stop going roon in circles and get tae the point!

How do you make a sausage roll?
Cheeky Wee Monkey: You push it doon the hill!

What's the difference between a ripe banana and a rotten banana?
Cheeky Wee Monkey: Six days!

Did you tell everybody I was an idiot?
Cheeky Wee Monkey: Aye, but ah didnae know it wis meant to be a secret!

What should you do if you break your leg in two places?
Cheeky Wee Monkey: Never go back tae these places again!

Why did the orange lose its job?
Cheeky Wee Monkey: It couldn't concentrate!

Why was the sword swallower sent to jail?
Cheeky Wee Monkey: He coughed an' killed six people!

What goes up in Scotland when the rain comes down?
Cheeky Wee Monkey: Umbrellas!

What do you call a spaceship which is hot inside?
Cheeky Wee Monkey: A frying saucer!

Why did the girl take a pencil to bed?
Cheeky Wee Monkey: So she could draw the curtains!

What do you do with a green monster?
Cheeky Wee Monkey: Wait until it ripens!

Why did the baby strawberry cry?
Cheeky Wee Monkey: Because its mum and dad were in a jam!

What washes up on small beaches?
Cheeky Wee Monkey: Microwaves!

If Martians live on Mars and Venusians live on Venus, who lives on Pluto?
Cheeky Wee Monkey: Fleas!

What is the centre of gravity?
Cheeky Wee Monkey: The letter 'v'.

What do aliens wear to posh weddings?
Cheeky Wee Monkey: Space suits!

What are aliens' favourite sweets?
Cheeky Wee Monkey: Martian mallows!

If you eat too much cake what do you get?
Cheeky Wee Monkey: Stomach-cake!

What do lawyers wear in court?
Cheeky Wee Monkey: Lawsuits!

What has four wheels, smells and flies?
Cheeky Wee Monkey: A dustbin lorry!

What do you call a popular perfume?
Cheeky Wee Monkey: A best smeller!

If Mr and Mrs Bigger had a baby, who would be the biggest of the three?
Cheeky Wee Monkey: The baby, because it's a little bigger!

Where do armies live?
Cheeky Wee Monkey: Up the sleevies o' yer jacket!

What's the best way to defeat your opponent?
Cheeky Wee Monkey: Cut aff his legs!

Why did the loaf go to hospital?
Cheeky Wee Monkey: He felt a wee bit crummy!

Why are aliens messy tea-drinkers?
Cheeky Wee Monkey: On flying saucers it's hard not tae spill it!

Why is it difficult to keep a secret in Scotland during the winter?
Cheeky Wee Monkey: Because yer teeth chatter!

Why don't sharks eat clowns?
Cheeky Wee Monkey: Because they taste funny!

What did one lift say to the other lift?
Cheeky Wee Monkey: Ah think ah'm coming doon with something!

What do you call a boomerang that won't come back?
Cheeky Wee Monkey: A stick!

Cheeky Wee Monkey: Ah fell aff a thirty foot ladder today.
I'm surprised you weren't killed.
Cheeky Wee Monkey: Och, ah only fell aff the first rung!

Why did the traffic light go red?
Cheeky Wee Monkey: You would too if you had tae change in the street!

What happened to the silly tap dancer?
Cheeky Wee Monkey: He fell intae the sink!

What is the difference between a buffalo and a bison?
Cheeky Wee Monkey: You cannae wash your hands in a buffalo!

Why are there so many McGregors in Scottish phone books?
Cheeky Wee Monkey: Because they all have phones!

What is the best way to keep fish from smelling?
Cheeky Wee Monkey: Cut aff their noses!

What gets bigger the more you take away from it?
Cheeky Wee Monkey: A hole!

What do you call a man with sports equipment on his head?
Cheeky Wee Monkey: Jim!

What happens if you cross a bridge with a car?
Cheeky Wee Monkey: You get tae the other side!

How did the mother burn her ear?
Cheeky Wee Monkey: She answered the iron!

How did she burn her other ear?
Cheeky Wee Monkey: They called back!

How did Darth Vader know what Luke Skywalker was getting for Christmas?
Cheeky Wee Monkey: He felt his presents!

Why could the seaman not play cards?
Cheeky Wee Monkey: He was sitting on the deck!

Why do bicycles fall over?
Cheeky Wee Monkey: Because they are two-tyred!

Where does a one-armed man shop?
Cheeky Wee Monkey: At a secondhand shop!

What do you call a girl on the horizon?
Cheeky Wee Monkey: Dot!

Why can't a girl ask her brother for help?
Cheeky Wee Monkey: Because he cannae be a brother and assist her too!

What did the hill say to the Scottish mountain?
Cheeky Wee Monkey: Hi Ben!

What did the North Sea say to the Atlantic Ocean?
Cheeky Wee Monkey: Nothing, it jist waved!

How do you make a bandstand in a park?
Cheeky Wee Monkey: Take away their chairs!

What did the wee angel die of?
Cheeky Wee Monkey: Harp failure!

What is a polygon?
Cheeky Wee Monkey: A parrot on its holidays!

How was the gypsy who won the lottery paid?
Cheeky Wee Monkey: In travellers' cheques!

Did you hear about the McDonalds on the moon?
Cheeky Wee Monkey: The Big Macs are great but there's no atmosphere!

Did you hear about the invisible man marrying the invisible woman?
Cheeky Wee Monkey: Their children are not much tae look at either!

Cheeky Wee Monkey: Did you know that the smartest person in Scotland is going deaf?
No, tell me about it.
Cheeky Wee Monkey: Pardon?

I've been teaching my dog to beg.
Is he any good?
Yes, yesterday he came home with £5.35p!

Did you hear about the man who stayed up all night to see where the sun went?
Cheeky Wee Monkey: It finally dawned on him!

Daddy, can I have an encyclopaedia?
No. You can walk to school like all the other children!

A hen walked into a jewellers shop and asked for a clock.
The jeweller produced a clock and said, "This is a clock made from gold. It is one thousand pounds."
"Too dear," said the hen.
So the jeweller produced a clock made of silver and said, "This clock is five hundred pounds."
"Too dear," said the hen.
The jeweller produced another clock and said, "This clock is made from wood and costs five pounds."
And the hen said, "A clockawoodeldo!"

What lies at the bottom of the North Sea and twitches?
Cheeky Wee Monkey: A nervous wreck!

Man to Cheeky Wee Monkey in an antique shop: How much are these antlers?
Cheeky Wee Monkey: Twenty pounds.
Man: They're affa dear.
Cheeky Wee Monkey: Did ye think they were affa a rabbit?

Cheeky Wee Monkey says: I'd like to go to Holland one day and see a clog. Wooden shoe?

Cheeky Wee Monkey says: If olive oil comes from olives, where does baby oil come from?

CHRISTMAS CRACKERS

Why does Santa go down the chimney?
Cheeky Wee Monkey: Because it soots him!

Which of Santa's reindeer has bad manners?
Cheeky Wee Monkey: Rude-olph!

Where did Santa go to learn to slide down chimneys?
Cheeky Wee Monkey: A chimn-asium!

What does Santa's cat want for Christmas?
Cheeky Wee Monkey: New claws!

What is Santa's wife called?
Cheeky Wee Monkey: Mary Christmas!

Who looks after Santa when he's ill?
Cheeky Wee Monkey: The National Elf Service!

What girl was born on Christmas day?
Cheeky Wee Monkey: Christmas Carol!

What do you get if you cross Santa with a duck?
Cheeky Wee Monkey: Christmas quackers!

What is Rudolph's favourite day?
Cheeky Wee Monkey: Red Nose Day!

What is the best Christmas present of all?
Cheeky Wee Monkey: A broken drum. You cannae beat it!

Why does Santa have three gardens?
Cheeky Wee Monkey: So he can Ho, Ho, Ho!

Who never eats at Christmas time?
Cheeky Wee Monkey: Turkeys, they're always stuffed!

How would you dismiss Santa?
Cheeky Wee Monkey: Give him the sack!

How do you eat your Christmas turkey dinner?
Cheeky Wee Monkey: Ah gobble it all down!

When does Santa say "oh, oh, oh?"
Cheeky Wee Monkey: When he's walking backwards!

What do elfs learn at school?
Cheeky Wee Monkey: The elfabet!

Knock, knock
Who's there?
Oakum.
Oakum who?
Oakum all ye faithful!

Knock, knock
Who's there?
Doughnut.
Doughnut who?
Doughnut open this present till Christmas day!

Knock, knock
Who's there?
Wenceslas.
Wenceslas who?
Wenceslas bus home?

Knock, knock
Who's there?
A wean.
A wean who?
A wean in a manger!

Who is Santa's most famous elf?
Cheeky Wee Monkey: Elfvis!

Knock, knock
Who's there?
Hosanna.
Hosanna who?
How's Sanna Clause going to get down our chimney? We don't have one!

What's brown and sneaks around the Christmas dinner table?
Cheeky Wee Monkey: Mince spies!

What kind of motorbike does Santa ride?
Cheeky Wee Monkey: A Holly Davidson!

What nationality is Santa Claus?
Cheeky Wee Monkey: North Polish!

What did Santa reply when his wife asked about the liquid running down the window?
Cheeky Wee Monkey: It's reindeer!

What did Santa say when the toys misbehaved?
Cheeky Wee Monkey: Ah, toys will be toys!

What's the difference between the English alphabet and the Christmas alphabet?
Cheeky Wee Monkey: The Christmas alphabet has Noel!

What happened to the man who stole a Christmas calendar?
Cheeky Wee Monkey: He got twelve months in jail!

What did Adam say on the day before Christmas?
Cheeky Wee Monkey: It's Christmas, Eve!

SPORTING JOKES

Why didn't the skeleton play for Hibs?
Cheeky Wee Monkey: His Heart wisnae in it!

When did the ghost score at football?
Cheeky Wee Monkey: When the ball went over the ghoul line!

Why did the referee speak to the chicken at the rugby match?
Cheeky Wee Monkey: Because he was fowling!

What do you call the monkey team which won the Scottish Cup?
Cheeky Wee Monkey: The Chimp-ions!

What's a golfer's favourite meal?
Cheeky Wee Monkey: Tee!

Why is Murrayfield so hot after each rugby match?
Cheeky Wee Monkey: Because all the fans leave!

Who in Scotland goes puttputtputtputtputtputtputt?
Cheeky Wee Monkey: A very poor golfer!

What do you get if you cross a tiger with a footballer?
Cheeky Wee Monkey: Ah don't know, but for sure naebuddy will tackle him!

Which creature is good at hitting a tennis ball?
Cheeky Wee Monkey: A bat!

Why do golfers in Scotland wear two pairs of trousers?
Cheeky Wee Monkey: In case they get a hole in one!

What is green, has six legs and is four metres long, and would kill you if it fell out of a tree?
Cheeky Wee Monkey: A snooker table!

What is a horse's favourite sport?
Cheeky Wee Monkey: Stable tennis!

What becomes of Scottish footballers when their eyesight starts to fail?
Cheeky Wee Monkey: They become referees!

Why don't most crisps run marathons?
Cheeky Wee Monkey: Because they're Walkers!

Why will Cinderella never play football?
Cheeky Wee Monkey: She keeps running away fae the ball, has the wrong footwear, and has a right pumpkin for a coach!

What do you get if you cross an insect with a dance?
Cheeky Wee Monkey: A cricket ball!

Why did the footballer cross the road?
Cheeky Wee Monkey: He wisnae very good at corners!

What do golfers use in China?
Cheeky Wee Monkey: China tees!

What do you call a pigeon who skis in Scotland?
Cheeky Wee Monkey: A skean dhu!

Why did the hen run onto the football pitch?
Cheeky Wee Monkey: Because the referee blew for a foul!

How do you spoil a footballer's birthday?
Cheeky Wee Monkey: Give him a red card!

What do you get if you cross a footballer with a mythical creature?
Cheeky Wee Monkey: A centaur forward!

Two cats had a boat race. One cat was called '123' and the other 'un deux trois'. Which cat won the boat race?
Cheeky Wee Monkey: '123' won, because un deux trois cat sank!

Why did the stupid racing car driver make twenty pit stops?
Cheeky Wee Monkey: He kept asking for directions?

What do you call a Scottish horse rider?
Cheeky Wee Monkey: Jock-ey!

What do you call the goalkeeper in the Scottish ghosts football team?
Cheeky Wee Monkey: The ghoulie!

Which footballer is the smelliest?
Cheeky Wee Monkey: The scenter forward!

What does the winner of every race lose?
Cheeky Wee Monkey: Their breath!

Why is tennis so noisy?
Cheeky Wee Monkey: Because all the players raise a racquet!

Why do Scottish footballers always make a mess of their jerseys?
Cheeky Wee Monkey: They cannae stop dribbling!

What do footballers and magicians like to do?
Cheeky Wee Monkey: Have hat tricks!

Which kind of footballer is best at lighting a match?
Cheeky Wee Monkey: A striker.

Which sport is very naughty?
Cheeky Wee Monkey: Bad-minton!

Why are footballers like fishermen?
Cheeky Wee Monkey: They're both happy when they've got a few in the net!

What sport do waitresses like?
Cheeky Wee Monkey: Tennis, because they usually serve so well!

YOU CAN'T POSSIBLY TELL THESE TO GRANDMA!

What did the submarine say to the Arran ferry?
Cheeky Wee Monkey: Ah can see yer bottom!

What happens if you fart in Holyrood Palace?
Cheeky Wee Monkey: The Queen gives you a Royal pardon!

What's the last thing that goes through a wasp's brain when it hits a car windscreen?
Cheeky Wee Monkey: Its bum!

What did the fish say when it hit a concrete wall?
Cheeky Wee Monkey: Dam!

Why do you call your dog Joiner?
Cheeky Wee Monkey: Because it does wee jobbies around the house!

What do you need to do if you crawl under a cow?
Cheeky Wee Monkey: You need to be careful, udderwise ye might get a pat on the heid.

Why are you taking so long in the toilet?
Cheeky Wee Monkey: Ah'm writing a poo-em!

Where do you find a dog with no legs?
Cheeky Wee Monkey: Exactly where ye left him!

What kind of button won't unbutton?
Cheeky Wee Monkey: A belly button!

Cheeky Wee Monkey: My baby brother just lost three pounds.
My goodness. Is he sick?
Cheeky Wee Monkey: No, my mother just changed his nappy!

How did they know that the man was eaten by a shark with dandruff?
Cheeky Wee Monkey: They found his Head and Shoulders on the beach!

What do you get if you cross a long-haired rug with an elephant?
Cheeky Wee Monkey: A great big pile in your living room!

What do you call a boy who has no underpants on?
Cheeky Wee Monkey: Nicholas!

What's the difference between a letterbox and a cow's backside?
Cheeky Wee Monkey: Well if you don't know I am certainly not giving you any letters to post!

What has two grey legs and two brown legs?
Cheeky Wee Monkey: An elephant with diarrhoea!

Why did Tigger look down the toilet?
Cheeky Wee Monkey: To find Pooh!

What do you get if you cross a boy who has just had an accident in his pants, with a dead owl?
Cheeky Wee Monkey: Someone who smells but doesnae give a hoot.

How many times do moon men go to the toilet?
Cheeky Wee Monkey: Only once in a loo moon!

How many times did the boy pass wind in school.
Cheeky Wee Monkey: Quite a phew!

Cheeky Wee Monkey: Can I go to the toilet, miss?
Not until you've said your alphabet.
Cheeky Wee Monkey: abcdefghijklmnoqrstuvwxyz.
Where's the 'p'?
Cheeky Wee Monkey: Running doon ma leg, miss!

What do you call a smelly Santa?
Cheeky Wee Monkey: Farter Christmas!

How do most toilets look?
Cheeky Wee Monkey: Flushed!

Which poo smells quite nice?
Cheeky Wee Monkey: Shampoo!

Why is the sand at the beach wet?
Cheeky Wee Monkey: Because the sea weed!

What did the nose say to the finger?
Cheeky Wee Monkey: Stop picking on me!

What has a bottom at the top?
Cheeky Wee Monkey: Yer legs!

The toilet seats were all stolen from a Scottish school.
Cheeky Wee Monkey: Well, now the children will have nothing to go on!

What is an Ig?
Cheeky Wee Monkey: An Eskimo's house withoot a loo!

What does a girl get if she pulls her knickers up to her armpits?
Cheeky Wee Monkey: A chest o' drawers!

Who shouted 'Knickers!' at the big bad wolf?
Cheeky Wee Monkey: Little Rude Riding Hood!

Why did the toilet paper roll down the hill?
Cheeky Wee Monkey: Tae get tae the bottom!

What is invisible and smells like carrots?
Cheeky Wee Monkey: Bunny farts!

What do you get if you cross a hen, a dog and a poo?
Cheeky Wee Monkey: A cockle, poodle phew!

Why do you have holes in your underpants?
Cheeky Wee Monkey: So ah can get ma feet intae them!

Is that perfume I smell?
Cheeky Wee Monkey: It is, and aye, you do!

Can we have a baby pig as a pet, mummy?
Don't be silly. Think of the smell
Don't worry. He'll soon get used to it!

What do you get if you cross a birthday cake with a can of baked beans?
Cheeky Wee Monkey: A cake that blows its own candles out!

Which vegetable is very rude?
Cheeky Wee Monkey: The pea!

If you're Scottish when you go to the bathroom, and you're Scottish when you come out of the bathroom, what are you when you are in the bathroom?
Cheeky Wee Monkey: European!

Why does Sarah always wear nappies to parties?
Cheeky Wee Monkey: Because she's a party-pooper!

Where do bees go to the loo?
Cheeky Wee Monkey: At a BP garage!

Knock, knock.
Who's there?
A bear.
A bear who?
A bear bum!

Please, miss, can I go to the toilet?
French teacher: Oui.
No, it's actually the other kind!

The lifeguard at the swimming pool blew his whistle and told the boy to stop weeing into the pool.
'But many people do it,' protested the boy.
'Aye, but not off the high diving board!'

AND THE FINAL KNOCK, KNOCK JOKE . . .

Knock, knock.
Who's there?
Saul.
Saul who?
Saul there is from Cheeky Wee Monkey!

CHEERIO!

AND FINALLY . . . THE BANANA POEM.

Pardon me for being rude,
It was not me it was my food.
Pardon me, excuse my manner,
It was not me but a banana.
Pardon me for having sinned,
It was not me it was my wind.
Pardon me for having rifted,
Bananas in my tummy shifted.
Pardon me, I need the loo,
Oh, something's coming . . . it's a poo.
Pardon me, the loo's my fate,
Oh, mummy, daddy . . . it's too late!